WINSTON MESKILL

HOW TO FIND YOUR OWN
IKIGAI

MASTER JAPANESE WISDOM WITH KAIZEN IN
21 DAYS

to Build Daily Habits, Balance Work and Personal Life, and Discover True Happiness

© **Copyright 2025 - All rights reserved.**

The content contained within this book may not be reproduced, duplicated or transmitted without direct written permission from the author or the publisher.

Under no circumstances will any blame or legal responsibility be held against the publisher, or author, for any damages, reparation, or monetary loss due to the information contained within this book, either directly or indirectly.

Legal Notice:

This book is copyright protected. It is only for personal use. You cannot amend, distribute, sell, use, quote or paraphrase any part, or the content within this book, without the consent of the author or publisher.

Disclaimer Notice:

Please note the information contained within this document is for educational and entertainment purposes only. All effort has been executed to present accurate, up to date, reliable, complete information. No warranties of any kind are declared or implied. Readers acknowledge that the author is not engaged in the rendering of legal, financial, medical or professional advice. The content within this book has been derived from various sources. Please consult a licensed professional before attempting any techniques outlined in this book.

By reading this document, the reader agrees that under no circumstances is the author responsible for any losses, direct or indirect, that are incurred as a result of the use of the information contained within this document, including, but not limited to, errors, omissions, or inaccuracies.

CONTENTS

INTRODUCTION	5
CHAPTER 1: The Essence of Ikigai	9
What is Ikigai?	11
The Science of Purpose	17
Embarking on Your Journey to Purposeful Living	21
CHAPTER 2: The Power of Kaizen for Transformation	25
Understanding Kaizen	27
The Psychological Benefits of Small Steps	33
Kaizen in Practice	44
CHAPTER 3: Finding Your Personal Ikigai	47
Self-Discovery Tools	49
The Four-Circle Framework	69
CHAPTER 4: Integrating Kaizen into Your Daily Routine	89
The Basics of Habit Formation	90
Small Steps for Big Changes	104

CHAPTER 5: Balancing Work and Personal Life with Ikigai 115

    Harmonizing Passion and Profession 116

    Creating Boundaries between Work and Life 121

CHAPTER 6: Practical Kaizen Strategies for Every Aspect of Life 127

    Kaizen for Personal Development 128

    Learn How to Be in the Present 139

CHAPTER 7: Overcoming Challenges on the Journey to Ikigai 143

    Dealing with Obstacles 144

    Finding Motivation When It Wanes 153

    Embracing Uncertainty 157

CHAPTER 8: The 21-Day Plan to Master Your Ikigai with Kaizen 161

    Week 1 — Laying the Foundation for Your 21-Day Journey 162

    Week 2 — Building Consistency: Essential Daily Routines for a Life of Purpose 170

    Week 3 — Expanding and Reinforcing: Sustaining Habits Long-Term 185

    Take that First Step Today 188

THANK YOU! 195

REFERENCES 197

INTRODUCTION

> *"Your purpose in life is to find your purpose and give your whole heart and soul to it."*
>
> - BUDDHA.

"I've done it all, Winston. I've achieved everything I ever wanted in this life - the marriage, the kids, the career - I have it all. But yet, I can't shake the feeling that something is missing. Am I not supposed to be happy by now?" My friend looked lost, devastated, and agitated as she sat there, slowly sipping her tea and staring into nothing as she pondered over her life.

From an outsider's perspective, my friend had it all. We'd just come from watching her speak at a top tourism conference in Dubai, where people were clinging to all her words, eager to become the aspirational success that she was. Hours later, the attendees had left, and we were having drinks overlooking the beautiful city - the view was just incredible. For many people, this sight alone would have been enough to make their day. But after the applause had died down and the night was settling in, my friend was becoming well too aware of something that many of us have faced - *questioning whether we are truly living in our purpose, why we are so unhappy with what we have, and whether our happiness lies in another path.*

As I sat there, I knew I could not fault her for feeling so lost. After all, just a few years before this meeting, I had been in the same boat. I was that hotshot in finance who knew everything and anyone - your go-to for investment tips. The money kept streaming in, the houses got bigger, and the vacations became more exotic. Yet, I felt empty and disconnected from the world. I thought that my purpose and happiness lay in pursuing my career and working like a horse to give my wife and kids everything they wanted. So, I gave it my all, thinking that the ends would justify the means - the problem was that two decades later, the end was nowhere in sight. It was disappointing, bewildering, and isolating - what was I doing wrong? I had followed the roadmap to success. On paper, I was the picture of success, but my life was nowhere near perfect, and I was tired of faking it.

It wasn't until an impromptu trip to Japan that I discovered the philosophies of Ikigai and Kaizen - they were so simple yet so complex, and they opened my eyes in a way I never could have expected, giving my life meaning and enabling me to find that thing that we all seek—*a purpose, a reason to get up in the morning, something that is uniquely personal to us—that missing piece.* I could finally stop walking down the cookie-cutter path that people thought was the key to a successful life. Best of all, I was finally at peace and could finally stop chasing after everything I thought would fill that gap.

INTRODUCTION

Seeing as you chose this book, I can only imagine that you, too, have been struggling to find meaning in your life. Maybe you feel like you are on a hamster wheel, always on the go but getting nothing out of your daily routines. Maybe you are like my friend - you have everything you thought you wanted but can't quite seem to feel fulfilled. Or maybe you are in the rat race like I was, amassing wealth but finding little to no satisfaction in your assets.

You are not alone.

The truth is that people are always looking for meaning, something that gives them satisfaction in their lives and helps them look forward to sunrises. In fact, a 2021 Lifeway Research study revealed that 57% of Americans try to find more meaning in their lives at least once a month, while another 21% seek this purpose weekly. But if people are working so hard to find an answer to their existence, how is it that they have yet to find it? Where's the answer they are seeking?

Well, I have good news for you. For starters, what you're looking for (*what we all want - the secret to happiness*) is not out of reach. If anything, by mastering a few principles, you will be shocked at how easily achievable this meaning can be. Secondly, by choosing this book, you have already made the first of the many important steps in finding your purpose. In this practical guide, you will find all the Japanese secrets of Ikigai and Kaizen, which I will explore in detail, ushering you into a world of time-tested and effective approaches you will use to create meaningful habits that will help you balance your career and personal pursuits! And third, in just 21 days (yes, you read that right), you can transform your life and open the door to long-lasting happiness.

All you need to do is to open your heart and mind to a new way of looking at things. I'm not asking you to backpack across Japan learning from the sages like I did or to enroll in a year-long course where you change everything about yourself. Not at all. All I want is for you to entertain the idea that your life could be very different in just 21 days. And this all starts with turning this page and learning everything there is to know about purpose and how you can find yours.

Enjoy your journey to a happier and more fulfilled you!

CHAPTER 1:
The Essence of Ikigai

"The two most important days in your life are the day you are born and the day you find out why."

– Mark Twain.

The story goes that a rich man in his sixties went on holiday to a small island. As he lay on the beach days in a row, he noticed a pattern that left him puzzled, to say the least. A local fisherman in his twenties would show up at around nine in the morning, spend an hour in the sea in his small boat, come back with a few fish in his net, and leave for the day. Driven by curiosity, the wealthy entrepreneur approached the fisherman, eager to hear how he spent the rest of his day. So, the young man told him that after leaving the sea, he would sell the extra fish, make a delicious meal for himself and his family, go dancing with his wife, watch the sunset, and spend the night with his loved ones.

Stunned, the rich man pointed out just how unambitious the young man was. After all, according to the entrepreneur, the fisherman should have spent more time at sea to get more fish, sold more fish, bought more boats, commercialized his business, and moved his headquarters to a bigger city—he had a full-on strategic plan for this lowly fisherman to become a dollar millionaire by the time he was in his sixties. After all, the rich man had used a similar strategy to build his wealth. He had started by working in a fashion store, saved enough to start a dropshipping fashion business, and now, he had distributors all over the world. That's how he could afford to take his private jet and come to this small island three times a year just to get a tan. So, why was this young man content with so little?

Unmoved by the plan, the young man asked, "**Then what?** What do I get in the end?" The rich man answered, "Then you can move to a small island, spend your day at the beach, go dancing with your wife, and spend more time with your loved ones…" His voice trailed off as he realized the irony of his strategic plan. The young man laughed it off and went on about his day—he was already living in his purpose. He would not have chosen any other way in ten, twenty, or thirty years.

Have you ever asked yourself, "**Then what?**" Many people put in a lot of time and work on things that will not give them what they truly want and need in the end. Unfortunately, without knowing your end goal, you cannot find satisfaction in your daily life. But where do you start? - We begin our journey by understanding **Ikigai**, the concept that will shape the rest of this book.

CHAPTER 1: THE ESSENCE OF IKIGAI

By the end of this 21-day plan, I want you to have a clear picture of your "**Then what**"? If you were to start living your best life today, what would you be doing at this very moment and why?

What is Ikigai?

"To live is the rarest thing in the world. Most people just exist."
                                        - OSCAR WILDE.

If you look at what drives most people in today's society, you come across schools of thought like hustle culture, going all in, and boss mode. It seems harmless enough. After all, people are just advocating for more productivity. But does this come at a price?

Well, in 1980, the life expectancy in Okinawa, Japan, was 84 years for men and 90 years for women. Fast-forward to 2020, and this figure had fallen to 80 years for men and 87 years for women! Of course, this is much higher than the 2020 life expectancy for the US, which was 76 years for men and 81 years for women (Ryall, 2022). Nevertheless, there is a glaring disparity between the 1980 and 2020 numbers. What's happening to this Japanese society?

The Power of Purpose:
The Impact of Ikigai on Longevity and Health

You see, the people in Okinawa have been able to live such long lives because of their traditional diets, emphasis on physical movement, strong connections with their communities, and, as you may already have guessed, **ikigai**. But with hustle culture and other Westernized ways of thinking taking root, younger people are spending less time on these basic yet important aspects of life and giving in to productivity-driven lifestyles. And the result? The younger population is now grappling with more cases of lifestyle diseases and increased stress levels. Without any interventions, this life expectancy will keep dipping - it's a cause for worry, not just in Japan but also in other regions that have previously had high life expectancy rates.

But what way of life has previously shaped Okinawa, and why must we hold on to it?

While it may seem like **ikigai** is the trendy term of the decade that will soon be a memory, it has been part of Japanese culture for centuries. There are many early mentions of it in historical texts dating back to the fourteenth century. But the reason you're hearing more about it now owes to its popularity since Mieko Kamiya wrote her book "On the Meaning of Life" in 1966, paving the way for other authors (like me) to explore this concept.

Plainly put, Iki means "life," while gai refers to "value." As such, ikigai translates to a reason for living or a sense of purpose. But it's not as simple as saying, "X gives me a reason for being." Instead, it ties to the four elements below:

- **What do you love doing?** - Think of something you are passionate about.

CHAPTER 1: THE ESSENCE OF IKIGAI

- **What are you good at doing?** Can you think of something in which you excel?

- **What does the world need?** - How do you add value to those around you?

- **What can you get paid for?** Can you make money from what you're doing?

The intersectionality of these elements pave the way for **passion, vocation, mission, and profession,** as I will explain in Chapter 3 and guide you to your ikigai.

The intersectionality of the elements that result in ikigai

Examples of Ikigai in Real Life

The idea in ikigai is to find something that aligns with the elements of passion, vocation, mission, and profession - Only then can you find something that fulfills you and gives you a reason to live. But let's be honest. While simple, this explanation can be confusing. So, I'll use examples from Japanese culture to show you how ikigai works in daily life.

Example 1: Feast your eyes on Ikebana, the art of flower arrangement. People who practice ikebana arrange flowers in ways that promote balance and bring out the natural beauty of their arrangements. It is a highly intricate process whose results are aesthetic arrangements that make people appreciate nature even more. For the practitioners, the fulfillment comes from the creative freedom and the joy they get to give to the world.

Example 2: Forget about four o'clock tea and have some sado. In Japan, the traditional tea ceremony (sado) is not just about preparing a sumptuous cup of tea and presenting it in memorable ways. Instead, it extends to preserving the cultural heritage. Everyone taking part in the tea ceremony gets to enjoy a sense of peace by stepping back into traditions, and those presenting the tea enjoy sharing their skills and passion with their guests.

See? When you look at ikigai as a way of life, it makes a lot more sense. *Find what you love and are good at doing, which is valuable to the world.* And the money? Most people find that financial gains are not a priority once they find their ikigai - they get enough fulfillment just from the freedom of pursuing

CHAPTER 1: THE ESSENCE OF IKIGAI

their passions and changing people's lives for the better with their abilities. Many people who practice Ikebana or hold traditional tea ceremonies do it just for the passion.

Does that mean you cannot get rich with ikigai? You can - after all, you will get paid for what you do if you do it well. Jiro Ono is an excellent example of this. He's a sushi chef who owns a Michelin 3-star restaurant in Tokyo. He loves making sushi, is incredibly good at it, makes people happy with his delicious meals, and is a successful business owner. So, in his pursuit of excellence, he's also become a household name that often appears in the media.

But it's not just about becoming the face of magazines. Ikigai works for people at all levels in their careers and businesses. Take my friend Yoshiko, for example. From the moment he was old enough to help in the kitchen, he loved making traditional Okinawan dishes, from soki soba to taco rice to goya champuru. He used this passion to start a small restaurant in his hometown, which is now the pride and joy of his family. All his siblings work in this family-owned establishment and derive evident satisfaction from being part of something that means a lot to them, not just for the income but also for the chance to share authentic, hearty dishes with their community. So, in Yoshiko's pursuit of sharing his passion with the local community, he's also found a way to make money.

So yes, as I have illustrated with Jiro and Yoshiko and will show with many other examples in this book, ikigai and money can go hand in hand. However, the goal in ikigai is not to go into boss mode or fall into hustle culture. Instead, it is to find a balance that makes your life worth living.

How the Japanese integrate Ikigai into routines

Your ikigai defines everything in your life, from the minute you get out of bed till you hit the sack at night. In Japan, people who have found their ikigai start their days by setting their intentions and ensuring their activities align with their goals and values. What's more, they do not rush out to start the day each morning. Instead, they take time to relax, be it sipping a steaming cup of tea, doing some yoga, or reading a book.

When they finally embark on their daily tasks, they focus on those that align with their ikigai. But alignment alone is not enough. They work to continuously better their abilities (*which is kaizen, as I will explain later*) to increase their life satisfaction. For example, if you can make good tea, why not try to make great tea? These small changes go a long way in increasing their fulfillment. They take classes, take up hobbies, read books, and pretty much engage in activities that better them as people.

Social connections are a key part of ikigai, as they fall under the "moai" concept that encourages communal support. The Japanese focus on building strong relationships that better the communities and offer each other emotional support. They make time for their loved ones, whether checking in on them or just meeting up for a cup of tea. It's no secret that having this support is integral to a long and happy life—any retirement home volunteer will tell you the same thing.

But emotional health is just one part of the picture. The Japanese devote time to making healthy meals and engaging in regular exercise. They keep things simple with fun activities like walking or group exercises. However, some may choose martial arts to keep the traditions alive. And for food? They go for veggies, white meat, and other nutrient-dense options.

Come to the end of the day, the goal is to unwind, take note of the daily successes and challenges, reflect on what requires change, and be grateful for another chance to live in their purpose. And doesn't that sound just so practical and fulfilling?

When you continuously engage in activities that align with your purpose, then every intentional thing you do, be it taking a walk or calling a friend, feels meaningful. And that's the goal of this book.

The Science of Purpose

"You don't decide what your purpose is in life; you discover it."

- Bob Proctor

When Nelson Mandela decided to fight for equality in South Africa, he gave it his all, finding resilience in walking in his purpose. But his fulfillment was not in the accolades he received. Instead, it was from the satisfaction of making a difference in people's lives. Elon Musk finds joy in pushing the boundaries of technology. From his innovations, it's clear that his passion derives value for the world. And when we look at Oprah, we can agree that she found her purpose in inspiring people through storytelling and philanthropy. She's also been open about the sense of purpose she gets from fostering positive changes in society.

So, are they happy? Good question. I cannot speak for these public figures as I do not know them personally; however, many people who find and follow their purpose get more satisfaction from their lives as they focus on doing the things that fulfill them. While not all of them become (or want to become) household names, research shows that not only are they likelier to live longer but also happier lives.

Welcome to the science of purpose!

What the Research Shows

Ask many people about their careers or lives, and they will spend hours going on and on about how badly things are going - the leaking roofs in their homes, the increasing insurance premiums, the traffic to work, the bad weather - everything is falling apart. Martin Luther King Jr. could have chosen to grumble about the sad state of affairs in his life as he advocated for equality and justice. After all, like any activist would tell you, his fight was not easy. But rather than give in to the setbacks, he often expressed happiness about the small achievements to the big ones. Knowing that he was walking in his truth was enough to motivate him to fight harder.

That's the difference that purpose makes. Studies have shown that purpose affects us in the following ways:

CHAPTER 1: THE ESSENCE OF IKIGAI

- **Longevity.**

    Multiple studies, including findings from a Harvard Health Study, have found that people who have a purpose tend to live much longer than those with little or no sense of purpose. In one JAMA Network Open Study, the risk of death was 15.2% lower for people with a strong sense of purpose. Another Clearvue Health Analysis found that having little or no purpose put people at a 2.43* risk of dying compared to people with a high sense of purpose (Bilodeau, 2019; World Economic Forum, 2024).

- **Physical health.**

    I mentioned that health outcomes in Okinawa have been falling since people took on faster-paced lives. Well, purpose has a lot to do with this. Research shows that people with a high sense of purpose are at lower risk of conditions such as heart disease, stroke, and sleep issues. Why is this? When you have something to live for, you align your lifestyle in a way that gives you the best chance of enjoying it - you take care of yourself (Mejia, 2017; Li, 2019).

- **Emotional wellbeing.**

    Studies show that the world has one thing in common. Regardless of where you come from, your culture, or income, people whose lives have meaning are happier and more satisfied. This satisfaction results in lower stress levels and less anxiety, which lowers the risk of sickness and injuries. What's more, studies have linked this emotional well-being to increased resilience, which helps people weather the storms in their lives (Ortiz-Ospina & Roser, 2024; CDC, 2024).

So, why does purpose affect you so much? It's all about the dopamine effect. When you have your ikigai and engage in activities that align with it or see progress stemming from your alignment, you feel good about yourself, which triggers the feel-good hormones in your system. Each time you experience this pleasure, you can't help but align your tasks with your ikigai even more because you know that a feeling of satisfaction awaits you. Eventually, these dopamine hits translate to a better mood that lowers your stress levels, alleviating feelings of anxiety and depression. While this does not mean that you will never face adversity, purposeful living builds you up mentally so that you can be more resilient and easily navigate setbacks. It's like working out but for your brain!

- **Relationships.**

    People whose lives give them meaning are more likely to engage with their communities. And as research has shown, social isolation can be as harmful as smoking 15 cigarettes a day. The more connected we are with our ikigai, the more we can connect with the world and the richer our lives can be (Ortiz-Ospina & Roser, 2024; Johnson, 2023).

As Oprah once said, *"There is no greater gift you can give or receive than to honor your calling. It's why you were born."* Research proves that she nailed it on the head. By sharing your gift with the world, you also get to better your emotional, physical, and social health - everybody wins.

Embarking on Your Journey to Purposeful Living

"The mystery of human existence lies not in just staying alive, but in finding something to live for."
- FYODOR DOSTOYEVSKY.

I read something the other day that spoke volumes to me. People quickly get angry over small things like cold cups of tea, train delays, and long queues. But they keep quiet when it comes to the things you would think would bother them - the dreams they abandoned, the years they have spent focusing on things that do not matter much. Perhaps it's just easier for people to vent over small things because it feels safer to express their disappointment over these things. After all, the alternative is for people to be honest with themselves and acknowledge that the problem is not in the train delay or the cold tea - the problem is that they don't even want to be on that train or in that queue. Their anger stems from the fact that they keep making decisions that keep propelling them in the wrong direction, but they do not know how to get back on track. So, instead of facing the fact that they are on the wrong track, they focus on the small stuff they can control - it's safer.

Anger displacement (redirecting your anger to things other than the actual cause) is a common setback when you are not living in your purpose. I was that person losing my patience over minor inconveniences because I did not want to admit to myself that I was unhappy and that nothing was fulfilling me anymore. If you've been displacing your anger a lot lately, it's probably a sign that you're not on the right path.

Worry not.

In the following chapters, I will teach you how to peel back the layers and figure out what makes you happy, how to nurture it, and how to find your way to your ikigai, pave the way for continuous improvement in different areas, and create a life that satisfies you in every possible way. Months from now, you probably won't even notice when the train is late!

TURN KNOWLEDGE INTO ACTION!

Reading about Ikigai and Kaizen is just the first step—**real transformation happens when you apply these principles.** To help you implement what you learn, I've created an **interactive workbook** filled with printable exercises, habit trackers, and self-reflection pages.

Scan the QR code now or follow the link to download your **31-page Ikigai & Kaizen Workbook** and start your journey toward a more purposeful, balanced life!

https://personalgrowthpages.com/winston-ikigai-workbook

CHAPTER 2:
The Power of Kaizen for Transformation

"Success is the sum of small efforts, repeated day in and day out."
- Robert Collier.

When things have been going well for a long time, it's easy to assume that the streak will continue such that you put minimal effort into improving. *If you've been doing great at work, you settle into your nice paycheck and just focus on getting work done, unbothered by signing up for new courses or seeking growth opportunities. If your health has been excellent, you start skipping regular checkups and shrugging off minor symptoms. If you've not had a traffic law violation, you stop paying as much attention to the road signs and rules.* After all, you've been smooth sailing. What can go wrong now? You're safe.

That's the definition of complacency, a false sense of security that comes when you feel content with what you have and don't want to try anything else. But while it might seem like being content is good, complacency is not about contentment. Contentment is all about being grateful for what you have now while being **aware** that you have room for growth - it seeks balance. Complacency **ignores** areas in your life that require attention and instead pushes you into a space where you are okay with what you have and have little motivation to pursue growth.

And here is the problem—one day, the illusion fades. You wake up and realize that while you were clocking in hours maintaining the status quo, things around you were changing. Your work skills became obsolete, your health suffered, your company lost market shares—the list goes on.

So, am I advocating for you to fall back into hustle culture? Quite the opposite. We can agree that hustle culture has its ills - but so does complacency.

As such, finding your ikigai is not just about resting in knowing that your life has a purpose. Instead, it requires you to work towards this purpose continuously, improving yourself little by little so that Tomorrow's You is a little bit better than Yesterday's You and far better than Last Year's You.

Brick by brick, you not only become a masterpiece but also build the skill set necessary to keep up with the dynamism of life - after all, **the only constant thing in this world is change**.

CHAPTER 2: THE POWER OF KAIZEN FOR TRANSFORMATION

Understanding Kaizen

"Kaizen and innovation are the two major strategies people use to create change. Where innovation demands shocking and radical reform, all kaizen asks is that you take small, comfortable steps toward improvement."

- ROBERT D. MAURER.

In 2023, Toyota sold 11.23 million cars worldwide. It had previously sold 10.5 million cars in 2022, 9.5 million in 2020, 8.42 million in 2010, and 8.35 million in 2008. In 2024, it remains the world's top-selling automaker, a title that is not easy to get but one that it has held on to for the fourth year in a row. So, what's the secret? Kaizen!

Kaizen refers to continuous improvement by making small yet impactful changes. And in Toyota, all operations align with this. Every employee has a role in identifying inefficiencies in the organization (such as defects in models and excess inventory), finding their root causes, and suggesting ways to improve these processes. The organization then works on implementing these improvements, thus finding the best practices to use to ensure the systems keep running and that it can avoid bigger issues in the long term that could impact its productivity. So, while other organizations are working on complete overhauls, Toyota sticks to what works, improving what requires change and keeping an open mind that helps it take up new ideas as they emerge. And that there gives it a competitive advantage.

It seems simple enough, does it not? Well, that's because it is, which makes it the perfect way to offer more value to the world, thus giving you more satisfaction in your purpose, as you will see as we embark on the 21-day plan.

From Post-War Periods to Personal Growth Strategies

World War II left Japan in a tight spot. Japanese manufacturers were grappling with limited resources and needed innovative ways to keep producing goods in line with the market demands. They soon realized that by eliminating waste and other inefficiencies in their processes, they could make do with what little they had. These practices soon became the norm in the industry, allowing the country to rebuild its economy one small change at a time. Later on, American statistician W. Edwards Deming brought in the Plan-Do-Check-Act (PDCA) cycle to better manufacturing processes. But his work was building on something that already existed - what he was doing was creating a framework that other businesses could borrow in their search for excellence. Slowly, other industries borrowed this concept, and you can now find it in use in various industries, from healthcare to hospitality to banking. Everyone values these small changes because they are not only practical but also highly impactful.

It's not just organizations that are adopting kaizen. Individuals are also using it to better themselves, one small step at a time - after all, people are also organizations that can benefit from continuous improvement. For example, Will Smith may already be one of the best actors in Hollywood. But this doesn't make him complacent. The star has been open about his dedication to learning from his failures and addressing his weak points through his daily habits, which help him improve incrementally and maintain relevance in a cutthroat industry.

But regardless of whether you are revolutionizing your business or setting your eyes on better well-being, the kaizen concepts remain the same. What are they?

- **Visualization.**

    In any kaizen organization, charts, graphs, and other visual tools remind the employees of the overall goals. For example, 3M (Minnesota Mining & Manufacturing), a FORTUNE Small Business, uses process flow diagrams to map out the steps for each manufacturing process. By looking at them, employees can quickly tell if they are in line with the organizational goals.

    How about you? What are you working toward? What's your "Then what?" When you can see what you want, it's easy to filter your priorities to match your goals. Then, everything else I talk about in this section will fall in line. In Chapter 3, I'll teach you how to create a vision board so you can have that visual picture of your "Then what."

- **System Creation.**

    Kaizen organizations seek consistency in their operations as this helps them figure out what needs improvement and what works. It's easy to do the same thing with your life. For example, if you are handcrafting cardigans, you'd find yarn and crochet materials, design patterns, and stick to a process. Only then can you figure out what's working and what needs changes, e.g., you may realize that you spend too much time creating new patterns, resulting in a backlog in orders. You would then focus on making the cardigans, carving out less time for design.

- **Self-Assessment.**

  As I showcased with Toyota, organizations that use kaizen focus on analyzing their processes to find underlying issues and resolve them. The goal is always to question whether their improvements add value to their customers. You, too, can use the same strategy in relation to your ikigai. Every day, compare your daily routine to your ultimate purpose. Are you on the right track? What can you do to progress?

- **Openness to Feedback.**

  When did you last ask for someone's input on your life? If you're the only one judging your progress, it's easy to miss out on glaring issues. Toyota's management knows this and banks on its employees to figure out what it's doing wrong and how it can improve. The same can work for you.

  Be open to constructive feedback from people you trust. For example, if you're trying to improve your baking skills and try new things, invite people to sample your recipes. You may not like hearing that your skills need some tweaking, but that's the only way you can offer more value and gain more satisfaction from your path.

- **Continuous Improvement.**

    In 1985, Coca-Cola wanted to beat Pepsi in their game, so it came up with a new formula. It was a radical change - and people hated it - they wanted the original formula and did not care about the market wars. Coca-Cola learned its lesson, stuck to its path, and focused on making small yet practical changes that have made it the global giant it is today.

    This approach also works wonders for people. Know what you want to achieve, then break it down into smaller goals you can meet by following a daily routine. Want to run a 5k? Start by jogging around the neighborhood for half an hour each day. These small changes add up to big things over time.

- **Commitment to Growth.**

    You will face many setbacks on your journey, and how you approach the challenges will determine whether you level up or stay the same. It's important to adopt a **growth mindset** where you embrace the challenges that come your way, seeing them as opportunities to learn more about yourself and get closer to your goals. Martin Luther King Jr. is an excellent example of someone who built resilience by learning from his failures and staying true to his path even in the face of challenges.

- **Curiosity Matters.**

    There is so much knowledge in this world that you can't *truly* know everything. But there is always room for learning. Nurture your curiosity by committing to learning something new each week. You can choose to read books, sign up for a class, try a new skill, or cook a new recipe - there's a lot to try. By opening your mind and heart to new things, you find opportunities you never knew could contribute to your ikigai. Moreover, your life becomes exciting as you always have something else to try in the offing.

As I write this book, I'm learning woodworking - and I can't wait to show off my table to whoever joins us for coffee next time.

- **Simplifying your Life.**

    How do you spend your time? Are you doom-scrolling social media for hours every morning? Are you hanging out with people who drain your energy? Reflect on your life, identify activities that do not add value to your life, and seek ways to eliminate or reduce them.

    For example, checking my email each time I get a notification distracts me from the task I am working on for at least five minutes. Eventually, I may spend over an hour just checking my emails, responding to them, clicking on links, calling people for clarification, and so on. What's more, I am not fully engaged in the responses as I am already occupied with another task. However, if I choose two 20-minute blocks daily to check my email, I can focus on understanding the contexts and responding effectively without alternating between emails and my work.

    How can you streamline your daily routine to focus on your top priorities?

CHAPTER 2: THE POWER OF KAIZEN FOR TRANSFORMATION

- **Finding Balance.**

    Mind, body, and spirit - these are the core focuses in your journey to ikigai. It's essential to balance your personal and work lives so that they intertwine without one taking over. Of course, sometimes, you will find that your work needs you more; at others, your personal needs will override your work commitments. But at the end of the day, you will want to find a balance that helps you be present in both spheres of your life.

Finally, be **grateful** for what you have and all that's working. Being present and acknowledging your progress rewards your soul and gives you that push you need to remain committed to your ikigai. As we embark on this 21-day plan, I will give you the tools to implement kaizen in your life so that everything will fall into place.

The Psychological Benefits of Small Steps

"Strive for continuous improvement instead of perfection."

- KIM COLLINS.

Two women wanted to start a baking business. Woman 1 was on the fence about it. She didn't have enough baking skills, lacked the money to open a shop, and did not have a ready market. So, she figured she would invest her time baking cakes for her family at home, fine-tuning her recipes, and saving money until she was ready. The years went by, her cakes got tastier, and her savings got bigger, but she still wasn't ready - she needed more time. Woman 2 was a true newbie in the baking business. She had the same challenges as woman 1 - low expertise, no financial capital, and nobody knocking on her door for pastries. But that did not matter - she knew that she could only actualize her dreams if she worked with what she had. So, she started by making plain cakes and advertising them on social media and to her friends, baking the orders from home. Slowly, she incorporated the feedback into her recipes and was soon making delicious plain cakes that people wanted for teatime. Then, she progressed to flavored cakes, trying one option at a time. Soon, people were ordering these in advance. In just months, she went from being just another cake enthusiast to becoming a reliable baker. And in two years, her bakery had come to fruition.

So, what makes these women so different? One allowed her fears to rule her path, while the other was willing to put herself out there and do what it took to be a success. Many people fall in the former category, hoping for the stars to align in their favor before they can embark on what they want. After all, taking that first step is scary - I felt the same way about writing my first book. But if you wait, you might do so forever and end up regretting your inaction.

Let me show you how kaizen (the art of continuous improvement) can help you offer value to the world even when you think what you have is not enough.

CHAPTER 2: THE POWER OF KAIZEN FOR TRANSFORMATION

Procrastination: Behold the Thief of Progress!

"It is not because things are difficult that we do not dare; it is because we do not dare that they are difficult."

- LUCIUS ANNAEUS SENECA.

Procrastination is a huge problem in our society - people put off what they need to do, choosing to work on other things that are often just distractions. If you are honest with yourself, there's probably something you have been putting off for a while. Maybe you have an idea for a business but have been assessing it for years, and you are somehow unable to take the next step. Perhaps you want to get fitter but are always telling yourself that you will sign up at the gym next week -it's been years now, and you're still waiting for next week. Or maybe you've been talking about trying a roti recipe for the past few months and even have the ingredients, but your weekends just fly by as you sit on the couch watching yet another series. Do any of these situations sound familiar?

Whatever you are putting off, you are not alone. Many people (me included) often struggle with procrastination. Unfortunately, the longer you put off something, the harder it becomes to achieve. Luckily, the way to avoid this pitfall is to figure out why it presents. Then, you can work your way through it by addressing the possible causes with practical solutions. So, why might you be holding back on what needs to be done? Research points to the following possibilities:

- **You are afraid of failing.** Have you ever wanted to work on something but thought you didn't have what it took to achieve it? Like woman 1, in my example, thinking that you will fail or make mistakes pushes you to avoid working on a task. After all, if you're not chasing your goals, you don't risk having your plans blow up in your face.

- **You have too much on your plate.** Sometimes, you want to do something, but it feels like climbing a mountain. For example, if you want to organize an event with 100 people, where do you start - catering, entertainment, venue? When you have a lot to work out, it's easy to take a step back, unsure where to start.

- **You lack motivation.** We've all had to work on boring tasks in our lives. Maybe it's taking out the trash, mowing the lawn, or sitting through an unnecessary meeting. When we are in such positions, it's easy to put off the tasks because we don't think they add any value to our lives. At the end of this section, I will show you how you can get past this hurdle.

- **You manage your time poorly.** You might think a task will only take a few minutes or hours of your time, so you focus on other things. Or you may get distracted by other things that grab your attention. By the time you get to the task, you may realize that you lack enough time, and that may scare you into not even trying at all.

- **You are stressed out or anxious.** When you're having a bad day, it's easy to seek relief from distractions. You can spend hours on the phone, catch up with your movie playlist, or do just about anything to escape what you are feeling. In such times, you may prioritize pleasure over getting work done, as it is your body's way of self-regulating.

Sometimes, procrastination is just out of habit. When you often put off tasks, you might find that your natural response to your priorities becomes to work on them at the very last minute. That's because, after a while, your brain starts to register the relief you get from avoiding tasks as a good thing. So, whenever you have something to work on, you feel the urge to put it off just to get that temporary relief, not knowing that you are feeding a risky pattern that could affect your life in various ways.

Rewiring the Brain Through Kaizen

"Action will destroy your procrastination."

- Og Mandino.

Say your purpose in life is to help people get fitter by simplifying workouts and teaching people about nutrition. You might aim at reaching ten million people. But if you look at this big goal, it's easy to feel overwhelmed. After all, how do you get to all these people? What platform can you use? - this is where people get stuck. They get so engrossed in their inability to match up to their overall goals that they forget that successful journeys start with a single step.

Kaizen grounds you by helping you focus on the small improvements that will result in big changes. For example, instead of looking at ten million people, focus on just getting ten. How can you get these people? You can go to the local gym, source contacts from your friends, or even use social media. With this manageable goal, you have a higher chance of being successful, which sets the pace for the following **outcomes** that make it easier for you to beat procrastination:

- **You become more confident.** Each time you make a small step that results in progress, you feel better about yourself. That fear of failure keeps getting smaller as you learn just how capable you are of succeeding. With the progress tracking tools, I will share in this 21-day plan, you can look back, see what you have done, and give yourself a well-deserved pat on the back. Nothing builds self-esteem like a series of accomplished mini-goals!

- **You build momentum.** In your quest for these tiny successes, you build habits you can rely on to improve your progress over time. For example, if you learn that you work better after a good night's sleep, your overall routine will hinge on this, enabling you to deliver value even with big tasks because you know what foundational routines work best. Later chapters will cover the value of habits in detail.

- **You enjoy more clarity.** When you are not focusing on that huge task in your future, you enjoy a sense of calm. It helps you direct your resources to what's right in front of you, which keeps you grounded and allows you to avoid elevated anxiety and stress levels.

CHAPTER 2: THE POWER OF KAIZEN FOR TRANSFORMATION

- **You boost your dopamine levels.** Your brain grows to think based on your cycles. The more you achieve small successes and celebrate them, the more you feel the urge to hit your goals. It gets you into an **action-reward cycle** that helps you keep up the energy even in the wave of obstacles.

- **You become more resilient.** You will encounter challenges even when working on smaller goals. But each time you overcome these obstacles, you will experience renewed belief in your strengths that will make you more resilient. So, as the challenges increase as you work towards your ultimate purpose, you will find that you are less tempted to step back from daunting tasks.

Taking one step at a time might seem like a cliché. However, the accumulative effect of small successes in the long term speaks for itself, not just in Toyota but also in successful people. Take Serena Williams as an example. You may know her today as a star on the tennis court. But she did not get here in one day. In her interviews, she has been open about her commitment to continuous improvement by setting smaller goals that inevitably got her to the top of her game. What's more, she adapted her playing style based on her opponents - if something wasn't working, she fine-tuned it over and over until it fit the bill.

With kaizen, you don't focus on the mountain in the distance. Instead, you focus on taking the first step, assessing how well you did that, and thinking of ways to make the second step even better. By the time you get to the foot of the mountain, you already have what it takes to climb it.

Beat Procrastination Using Simple Techniques

Alyce P. Cornyn-Selby once stated, "**Procrastination is, hands down, our favorite form of self-sabotage.**" Yet doers like Woman 2 manage to break free from its hold. Here are some effective tools you can use to push through what you have been holding back from doing:

Exercise 1: Simplify Your Goals.

Work with your goals using the SMART approach as follows:

- **Specify** what you want.
- Make the goal **measurable**.
- Ensure the goal is **achievable**.
- Make it **relevant** to your purpose.
- Set a **time** limit to achieve it.

For example, you can state your goal as "I want to make four full-length adult cardigans within 28 days" as part of your larger plan of becoming an expert crochet artist.

Then, take your goal and break it down into smaller steps as follows:

- What must you do every week to get closer to your goal? E.g., put the panels together to complete a cardigan.
- What must you do every day to reach your goal? E.g., knit one panel each day.

CHAPTER 2: THE POWER OF KAIZEN FOR TRANSFORMATION

Your smaller goals will feed into your bigger ones to help you reach your final goal. With the SMART approach, you can use the smaller goals to track your progress, e.g., checking if you have made one panel each day.

Chapter 4 will cover more on how you can check your progress.

Exercise 2: Establish a Simple Routine.

What must you do every day to hit your daily goals? For example, you may find that you need five hours a day to finish a panel. As such, you would create a routine that ensures you get these five hours while leaving room for other important things in your life.

I will share more about this in the daily routines in Chapter 8.

Exercise 3: Use The Two-Minute Rule.

This approach has two sides, as follows:

- **For a small task.** If you can get it done in under two minutes, do it now.

- **For a big task.** If you think a task is challenging, work on it for two minutes at first. You will find that you have built some momentum after these two minutes. Use this to keep working on the task. For example, if you need to work on a 10-page proposal and your goal is to finish one page a day, start by working for two minutes and then use that momentum to complete the page for the day.

It works for everything, even housework!

Exercise 4: Avoid or Eliminate Distractions.

Create a space that encourages you to work and has few distractions. For example, if you often scroll the news, put your phone away or install an app that limits your phone usage. If you often get distracted by people around you, find a quiet place to work or wear headphones. Identify and address your weak points so you can focus on what is at hand.

Exercise 5: Make Boring Tasks Enjoyable

Doing the dishes, taking out the trash, calling customer care representatives who take hours to give you an answer - these are all examples of things you may want to postpone. But there are ways you can accomplish these boring tasks without feeling like you are taking years off your life. For example, I don't like doing the dishes, so I make it fun by listening to a podcast or nice music. When I have this entertainment, just you try to get between me and those dishes. My wife likes making a game out of folding laundry. She builds forts, color-codes the shirts, and dunks some clothes in the wash basket as she sings made-up songs. It's all a game to her, and she can spend an hour doing this.

CHAPTER 2: THE POWER OF KAIZEN FOR TRANSFORMATION

Here are examples of ways to make your tedious tasks more fun:

- **Make a game out of it.** For example, you can dare yourself to finish the task in five minutes and reward yourself with a treat if you succeed.

- **Work with a friend.** Sometimes, if the company is not distracting, it may push you to work harder. For example, my kids love doing their assignments in the same room - being in the same space with someone who's also working on a project motivates them to keep going.

- **Listen to music, a podcast, or an audiobook.** Audio entertainment is a great way to keep your head in the game while ensuring you enjoy the entire process.

Also, reward yourself for completing those boring tasks. For example, if you've been wanting to catch a movie with your friends, promise yourself that you will only do this after you have crossed off all your repetitious tasks for the week - it is a huge motivator!

Then, using the kaizen principles discussed in the previous section and the tools I will share in Chapter 4, find ways to improve your work continuously. See? Anything can seem doable if you break it down enough and implement measures to boost your productivity.

Kaizen in Practice

*"If you always do what you've always done,
you'll always get what you've always got."*

- Henry Ford.

Human lives are multidimensional, and the only way to truly lead a balanced life is to recognize the importance of caring for all these dimensions. But which are they, and how does kaizen play a role in bettering them?

The physical dimension encompasses your physical well-being. And let's be honest, this lays the foundation for your other dimensions. With continuous improvements, you can improve your well-being to provide more support for your other dimensions. For example, if you barely work out, you can challenge yourself to go on short walks in the evenings, which can gradually increase in complexity and duration over time. If your diet mainly consists of fast foods, you can start by making one healthy meal a day before moving to healthier meals on a regular basis.

The intellectual dimension focuses on your cognitive skills that shape your ability to think, reason, and learn. You can boost this through incremental learning and development. For example, you can carve out time to learn a new skill, practice another language, try a new musical instrument, or just about anything that challenges your cognitive skills. Part of leading a purposeful life is being open to continuous learning, as stated earlier in the Kaizen foundational principles.

CHAPTER 2: THE POWER OF KAIZEN FOR TRANSFORMATION

The mental dimension looks at how well you can handle various emotional and psychological situations. You can improve your mental well-being by taking steps such as carving out enough time to rest each day, opening up about your feelings, seeking therapy, journaling about your day, and seeking productive outlets for negative emotions.

The emotional dimension looks at how well you can understand and express emotions. It affects how well you respond when faced with challenges. By practicing mindfulness (e.g., with meditation), you can embrace gratitude and learn how to process negative emotions without letting them spill over into your life or affect your balance. Over time, this continuous connection helps you tap into a sense of calm that lowers your stress and anxiety levels.

The social dimension explores how we interact with other people, be they our friends, family, or community. In line with the "moai" concept in ikigai, it's important to nurture these relationships as they provide us with emotional support. You can use kaizen to foster these relationships by working on your communication skills, carving out time to spend with your loved ones, and reading books on how to be a better friend, family member, or community member.

The spiritual dimension relates to your connection to something that gives meaning to your life. While ikigai is a big part of this, many people also find meaning in their beliefs. Seek a way to connect with what adds value to your life, e.g., if you follow a religion, you can spend time exploring ways to connect with your religious beliefs even more. In this case, I will use ikigai as the guide. By following the steps in this 21-day plan, you can inch closer to your purpose and gain more satisfaction from your life.

The vocational dimension, which is what most people often look at, refers to your professional life. Kaizen helps you be more purposeful in your career or business by helping you manage your time and tasks better. For example, you can work on improving your productivity by using the two-minute-rule I discussed in the previous section or complete more tasks by working with a routine.

The environmental dimension looks at your impact on your surroundings. You can make small changes to improve this effect, such as recycling containers, turning off lights when not using them, switching to energy-efficient bulbs, and buying clothes from thrift stores. There are many practical ways to have a positive impact.

Since our lives are multi-dimensional, you cannot pick and choose what to focus on - all these aspects require you to put in an effort; otherwise, you lose out on the balance that is key to achieving your ikigai. However, the amount of work required will differ from one aspect to the other as you may find that you struggle more in some areas. For example, you may find that you are great at conserving the environment but have trouble maintaining good relationships. But, like I said at the beginning of this chapter, complacency is never the answer. So, even if you think you are doing great in one area, there's always room for improvement - the next chapters will show you how to achieve this growth in all these dimensions and how it ties to your overall ikigai. Let the journey begin!

CHAPTER 3:
Finding Your Personal Ikigai

*"Purpose gives meaning to our being,
and purpose has myriad meanings for us."*

- Somali K. Chakrabarti.

"What's the one thing you would spend time doing if you never had to worry about money?" That was my question to a group of servers I had met during an event prep to celebrate a friend's birthday - he was turning 45 and wanted to go big. The supportive friend I was, I showed up two hours early to help him share the live location with the guests, so I sat in the corner and texted away. From this vantage point, I could hear the servers grumbling about the long hours, their financial commitments, how they needed more money - you get the gist.

After a while, I engaged them in their conversation, trying to understand what they *truly* wanted. They all chipped in, talking about how more pay could help them accomplish more in life.

But when I asked them what they would spend their lives doing if money was no longer a concern, some muttered a few things under their breath, others just opened their eyes wider, while others just laughed - my question didn't make sense to them. They had never thought of doing anything else other than working. Their lives revolved around their jobs - they would make money, spend it on what they needed and wanted, run out of money, and make more, and the cycle continued. This was life as they knew it - it was what everyone around them was doing and would continue doing to survive. The concept of waking up and just doing something they loved - well, that was too foreign to envision. They did not even want to indulge me in it, terming my thinking as too unrealistic for this world. "What's the point of building castles in the air?" That pretty much summed up one server's thoughts as he walked away to finish another task on his list.

Unfortunately, many people are the same way. They choose their paths in life with money as the goal. But here's the problem. If they want $1,000 and get it, the satisfaction dies down really fast, and they think the answer lies in $10,000. They get that, but once again, the satisfaction fades, so they go for $100,000, then $1,000,000, then $10,000,000 - the quest never ends as they think that the reason for their dissatisfaction is their account balance - they always need a little more. So, give these people all the money in the world, and they will no longer have direction in life.

I pose the same question to you right now. What would you do with your life if money was no longer a concern? While ikigai encompasses money (vocation), this is but one part of leading a balanced life. For example, many people can get paid for what they are doing right now for work. What's more, they are good at it (profession), and the world needs their skills (mission). However, they do not love doing it and don't gain satisfaction from it. That's why they choose money as their goal.

How about we turn that around by discovering what you love doing (your passion) and how you can make this the core of your ikigai? Let's explore why you are truly on this earth. Hint - it's not for the money, but you might find that your purpose also turns you into the next Warren Buffet!

Self-Discovery Tools

"The things you are passionate about are not random; they are your calling."

- FABIENNE FREDRICKSON.

A 2024 report on the working-age population in the US revealed that 70% of this population was actively seeking a change in their careers due to dissatisfaction with their current career tracks (Apollo Technical LLC, 2024). Do you know why many people are stuck in dead-end careers or run businesses that they do not like? Well, it's very easy to find things you are good at that add value to the world, from which you can generate income. But it's very hard to nurture affection for something that does not fulfill you as a person.

The only way to avoid being stuck in this loop of continuous questioning and jumping on whatever sounds like a good deal is to uncover what you really care about. So, in this section, I will take you through the key exercises to find your passions in life, which we will use to hone in on your purpose in the next section. Take a deep breath, get comfortable, and open your heart and mind as we are about to get personal and honest.

Note: All the exercises in this section are key to finding your passions. Please review and complete them all, as they tie together and will be integral to all the other sections in this book.

Exercise 1: Reflective Journaling

The average person has several passions. You may even find that you feel passionate about ten things right now. Reflective journaling helps you figure out the passions that hold the most value in your life so you can get closer to choosing what you should focus on - Here's how you do it:

1. **Morning intentions (5–10 minutes).** Each day, write down the things you are most excited about trying or doing, whether or not you think it relates to your purpose. For example, you may be eager to try a new cake recipe, catch up with friends, join a Zumba class, etc.

2. **Midday reviews (5-10 minutes).** As the day ensues, keep note of everything you have experienced and how it has made you feel. What have you enjoyed the most?

What has made you feel fulfilled? Rate them out of 10 based on how you feel.

3. **Evening assessments (10-20 minutes).** Write down the highlights of your day, paying attention to what you enjoyed the most. It may even be things that you had not anticipated yet loved doing. Again, rate them out of 10.

4. **Weekly reflections (10-20 minutes) and experimentations.** Review your journal at each end of the week to see if any patterns are present in the ratings. Highlight the activities with the highest ratings and carve out time to explore them more the next week. For example, if you realize you enjoyed teaching your friend how to manage her money, schedule this with another friend the next week. This continuous exploration will help you figure out if you are truly passionate about something or just happened to have a good time with it during the week.

Exercise 2 on meditation will help you tap into these interests in more detail. In contrast, Exercise 3 will walk you through how to create an inventory to categorize them.

5. **Monthly reviews (20-30 minutes).** Look at the previous weeks and single out any evident patterns. Choose the activities that continuously rank high , and add in any new passions you have found along the way. Then, carve out time to explore them further.

Journaling like this helps you tune in to your actual passions over time, guiding you on what actually fulfills you.

Here's an example that you can use:

PROMPTS	EXAMPLE	EXCITEMENT LEVEL
MORNING		
What am I looking forward to doing today the most?	I'm eager to make an Instagram reel about my latest trip.	8/10
Why do I like it?	I love sharing my travel experiences with other people.	9/10
MIDDAY		
What have I enjoyed doing so far?	I loved getting positive feedback on my reel.	10/10
Why did I enjoy it?	People found it really informative, which made me happy - I added value to their lives.	10/10
EVENING		
What are the highlights of my day?	Creating my new Instagram reel and getting good feedback.	10/10
	Teaching Laura how to use the 50-30-20 budgeting principle	9/10
Did I learn anything new about my passions or interests?	I learned that I have a lot of financial knowledge to offer.	9/10
WEEKLY		
Which interests have appeared most in my journal this week?	Creating Instagram reels.	9/10

Why have I enjoyed them?	Reels – they help me connect with the travel community, which allows me to share what I love doing.	9/10
What do I want to explore more next week?	Make more reels.	10/10
	Teach my friends how to budget. I'm nervous about it.	8/10
MONTHLY (REFER TO EXERCISE 3)		
What patterns have I seen this month?	I get excited each time someone says that my reels have impacted them positively.	9/10
	I love it when my friends learn something new about finances in our talks.	9/10
What interests do I want to pursue more?	I want to enroll in financial courses to learn more skills so I can teach more people, not just my friends.	10/10
What goals can I set to help me improve?	I want to get a new camera to take better videos so I can make more reels.	9/10
	Finish a finance master course in 1 month.	9/10

Tips for Insightful Journaling.

While journaling is an effective approach to finding your passions, it only works if you are honest and consistent. Stick to the prompts in this exercise, ensure you write down something every day, and most importantly, be honest with yourself. It's about finding your purpose, and only you can truly know how you feel about what you are doing.

The next exercises will offer insights that will align your journaling with the interests that could shape your ikigai.

Exercise 2: Self-reflection

Are you unsure what you are truly passionate about and what you do out of obligation, habit, or other reasons? Meditation helps you work through the noise and connect with your passions. Here's how you can achieve this:

1. **Set out 15 to 30 minutes each week** as part of your routine. Please note that this exercise works in conjunction with the weekly assessment in **Exercise 1**.

2. **Sit or lie down in a quiet spot** where you can relax without getting disturbed or distracted. It can be the floor of your bedroom, under a tree in your yard, or any other place where you feel comfortable letting go of your guard. Also, put your phone on silent mode and get rid of any distractions near or around you.

3. **Take some deep breaths.** Meditation only works if you relax your body and mind. You can achieve this by breathing in through your nose and allowing the air to fill your lungs so that your stomach rises. Then, hold this breath for a few seconds before exhaling with your mouth, concentrating on the movement of your chest as you let go. Repeat this about five times until you start feeling relaxed.

4. **Close your eyes and imagine yourself in your happy place.** A happy place is a real or imagined place that makes you feel happy and settled as all your problems fade away - It can be anywhere. For me, that place is when I am walking on the beach at sunset. The sound of the crashing waves, coupled with the view of the orange glow from the setting sun, just makes me so happy – it's indescribable. For my wife, this place is the local hiking trail, which has a meadow with a stream. She loves how peaceful and beautiful it is that she sometimes spends hours here, napping, knitting, reading a book, you name it.

What's your happy place? Allow your mind to take you there, take in the vision, and imagine yourself spending time here. What are you doing in this happy place? Why does it make you happy?

5. **Think of other things that bring you joy.** Now that you've tapped into the wholesome happiness you get in your happy place think of other things that make you happy and imagine yourself doing them. Be honest with yourself by following the prompts below:

    - What activities genuinely make me happy even when nobody is watching?

    - If I had to spend 6 hours doing something without any breaks, what would it be?

    - Why do I like this activity so much?

- What am I good at doing that other people have a problem achieving?
- If I no longer had to work for money, what would I spend my time doing?
- What have I always been curious about trying but did not out of fear?

6. **Use online passion assessment tools for brainstorming.** Sometimes, you may forget about things you actually enjoy or are interested in - So, to ensure you do not leave anything out, go online and search for a passion assessment tool. It will give you prompts that will guide you on things that actually might interest you or already fascinate you. Add them to the list.

7. **Go back to exercise 1 on journaling.** Look back on your week and think of all the things you have been doing. Then ask yourself the following questions:

  - Have I been doing any of the things that make me happy? If so, which ones? If not, why not?
  - What passions can I explore next week?

You will need to be honest with yourself. For example, you may find that you are good at dancing and it makes you happy, but you avoid doing it because you care too much about what people think. We all hold back from living our best lives for different reasons. With meditation, you can question your stance on your approaches and think of whether you are sabotaging yourself knowingly or unknowingly. Then, work on a routine that allows you to explore your passions more, as this will help you use **exercise 1** to figure out what truly fulfills you.

Exercise 3: Interest Inventory

From your reflective journaling and meditation, you will have a good idea of what things interest you. But how actionable are they per your ikigai? Well, that's where this exercise comes into play. Each week, as part of your journaling, you will create an inventory that helps you rank your interests to hone in on what matters the most. How?

Step 1: Take Stock of All Your Interests.

   a. **Refer to exercises 1 and 2 to identify your current interests,** be they hobbies you enjoy, topics you are curious about, or aspects you love discussing. Note them down.

   b. **Look back at your interests as a child or teenager.** Are there things you did back then but have now stopped doing? What did you love doing and why? Are you still curious about them? Add these to your list.

   c. **Highlight your curiosities.** Are there any subjects you want to research more? What activities would you like to try? Think of anything that has crossed your mind over the years. For example, maybe you have always wanted to learn how to play the piano but stopped because you thought you would not hack it. Write down all these aspirations.

Step 2: Weigh Your Interests against Your Abilities.

    d. **Review your current skill sets.** Exercise 4 will walk you through how to do this to assess what talents come naturally to you and how you can rely on these in shaping your journey.

    e. **Think about your value systems.** What are your beliefs and values? Where do they stem from, and what biases may inform them? Do your interests align with these values? We all have values that inform our decisions such that when we adopt lifestyles that do not align with these beliefs, we feel out of place. For example, you may love fashion hauls. However, you care deeply about the environment, and buying fast fashion leaves you feeling guilty. So, what values are important to you, and how can they impact your interests?

    f. **Examine how you feel about the activities that remain on your list.** Some may leave you wanting more, while others may frustrate you to some extent. Go through the list and rate each activity based on the level of excitement you get from it.

Step 3: Review Your Outlook

    g. **Assess the satisfaction you get from the remaining interests when faced with challenges.** Say, for example,

CHAPTER 3: FINDING YOUR PERSONAL IKIGAI

that you love making organic lotions. However, any time you make a bad batch, you get frustrated and want to give up. Can you imagine yourself turning this into a long-term activity? Probably not. Think of the challenges you face with each item on your list, how you handle the challenges you face and how you feel once you get past the hurdles. If you often stick to the plan and end up feeling fulfilled after solving the issue, you've got gold.

The next step is to try all the activities remaining on your list each week to gauge how you feel about them using the prompts in **Exercise 1**. Soon enough, you'll have a clear idea of the interests that speak to who you are.

Use the table below as a reference.

STAGE	ACTIVITY		
	TAKE STOCK OF ALL YOUR INTERESTS		
1	What are my current interests? e.g., styling people, dancing, cooking, sharing relatable stories, etc.	What did I enjoy as a child or teenager but have stopped doing, though it makes me happy? e.g., going on hikes, baking fresh cookies, etc.	What things am I curious about learning? e.g., learning to play the piano, making NFT art, etc.

2	**GAUGE YOUR ABILITIES**		
	What things am I naturally good at in relation to my interests?		
	e.g., I have an eye for fashion and can turn bland clothes into fashion statements.		
	What values do I have that could affect my ability to pursue my interests?		
	For example, I believe in environmental conservation and do not support fast fashion, but I cannot afford ethical clothing.		
	How much excitement do I get from each interest on my list?		
	e.g., Dancing – 10/10, cooking – 8/10, styling people 9/10.		
3	**REVIEW YOUR OUTLOOK**		
	ACTIVITY	HOW I FEEL ABOUT CHALLENGES	HOW I FEEL AFTER SUCCEEDING
	Cooking	4/10	8/10
	Making bags	8/10	10/10

Every week, you will embark on the activities that have passed the first two stages. Then, you will review them (stage 3) per the prompts in **Exercise 1**. Soon enough, you will have a handful of activities that align with you in every which way.

Exercise 4: Strengths and Skills Analysis

Ikigai works like a two-way street in that you offer value to the world, and the world repays you. For example, when Oprah

CHAPTER 3: FINDING YOUR PERSONAL IKIGAI

talks about social issues, she empowers people who are going through similar circumstances. In return, she gets to live in her purpose, which gives her satisfaction. But this only works because she's invested in her natural knack for storytelling, an innate strength. The same applies to all other ikigai examples you will come across - you have to zero in on what's special about you, as this helps you make the most of your passion such that you can offer the most value, which will, in return, give you the most satisfaction. In business, we call this a competitive edge.

How do you find your edge? The idea is to analyze your current strengths and weaknesses and determine whether they can support the interests in your inventory. In this case, I will use the example of Mary. She is a stay-at-home mum who wants to understand and pursue her purpose. Here is how she goes about the process and how you, too, can analyze yourself:

Step 1: Perform a self-assessment. Everyone has things that come naturally to them - these are your strengths. At the same time, there are areas where you face difficulties, yet other people have an easy time. For example, Mary is an excellent cook, can make a good meal from almost anything, and is great at keeping time. But she struggles with taking constructive criticism and has a hard time saying "no."

Step 2: Ask for feedback. While you think you know everything about yourself, other people around you also note your strengths and weaknesses. For example, my wife can easily point out my blind spots, which I may not easily see because of my biases. Find people around you who you trust and ask for their insights on what makes you great and what you need to work on—friends and family are a good place to start.

In Mary's case, her friends and family think that she shows a lot of promise in her cooking abilities, her ability to manage her household without extra help, and her dedication to her loved ones. But they think she pushes herself too much, is highly sensitive to feedback, and is too much of a perfectionist.

Step 3. Analyze your opinions and those of your loved ones. Are you seeing any patterns? Take note of the strengths and weaknesses that often come up. For example, from Mary's analysis, we can see that she excels in cooking and organization. Still, she struggles with taking time for herself or accepting feedback from other people.

Step 4. Go back to exercise 3 and relate these strengths and weaknesses with your interests. Are they helping or hurting your chances? The goal at this point is to assess where you are and what requires changes for you to succeed in improving – remember that we are working to avoid complacency in all aspects of our lives.

Mary, for example, loves making meals for her loved ones and can spend hours in her day recreating recipes. With her strengths in cooking and organization, she can excel in turning this passion into her purpose, as I will later explain in the next section.

Step 5. Work on bettering yourself by making small yet impactful changes. **Chapter 4** will teach you how you can

CHAPTER 3: FINDING YOUR PERSONAL IKIGAI

leverage your strengths and work on your weaknesses to help you pursue your passions. For example, Mary may be a great cook, but her perfectionism can get in the way of sharing this skill with other people. She'd need to address this moving forward, as I will explain in Chapter 4.

Use the table below to help you note down everything you learn. I will use Mary's example to get you started. Can you use her lead to review your strengths and weaknesses?

STAGE	STRENGTHS	EXAMPLE	WEAKNESSES	EXAMPLE
SELF-REVIEW		I am an amazing cook. I am great at managing tasks.		I do not respond well to criticism. I am unable to say "no" to people who need me.
FEEDBACK		I make delicious meals. I run an organized household. I am dependable.		I am too much of a perfectionist. I stretch myself too thin.
ANALYSIS		I am great at cooking and organization.		I have people-pleasing habits, and I am highly sensitive to negative feedback.

This analysis will give you more insights into where you shine and areas where self-improvement is necessary. In the next section, I will show you how to compare your strengths and weaknesses to possible vocations and professions so you can land on something that you not only love but can excel at. **Chapter 4** will offer more insights into self-improvement. For this exercise, you can focus on these three stages.

Exercise 5: Visualization

Remember the vision board I mentioned under Kaizen visualization practices? Well, we are about to make one. Trust me - this is a fascinating process that my children also enjoy. Each year, this is how we map our resolutions! So, how does it work?

Step 1: Calming Your Mind.

Visualization enables you to imagine your perfect life if everything were to fall into place. So, you don't want distractions or anxieties getting in the way. You can create the ideal environment in the following ways:

- Choose a quiet spot in a comfortable area where you can sit or lie down.

- Take a few deep breaths, inhaling through your nose and exhaling through your mouth. As you do this, concentrate on the flow of the air and the movement of your stomach. How does it make you feel? Keep at it for a few minutes until you feel calm.

- Focus your mind on the goal of this exercise – it's all about figuring out what makes you happy when you have no obligations to worry about or people to please.

It will take a few minutes for you to clear your mind – there is no rush.

Step 2: Picturing Your Perfect Life

Imagine if you woke up today and could do anything you wanted, as money was no longer a concern. *What would that day look like? What would you do? Who would you want there?*

For example, you could spend the morning drinking fresh coffee as you bask in the sun, take a walk with your dogs, stop by the market for fresh fruit, hang out with your friends, spend the evening preparing pasta with sauce, and tuck your kids into bed by reading them their favorite stories.

What's your version of a perfect day?

Now, imagine you could do what you wanted every day for a week. What would change? How about if you had the whole year?

Exercises 1, 2, and 3 will give you insights into the activities that excite you the most. Can you picture yourself doing these in the future? How do you feel about the prospect of waking up every day and doing those activities? Note down the ones that bring you the most fulfillment and would fit right into this long-term plan.

Step 3: Turning Your Vision into Reality

When you have a visual of what your perfect life entails, you feel the motivation to work towards it. To take this motivation to the next level, how about we make a vision board that showcases everything you love?

A vision board has two main features:

    a. **Segments:** These are the key areas of your life that intertwine to contribute to your overall well-being. Think of what matters to you in each segment and write it down.

    b. **Vision:** This is what you want your life to look like.

Let's use Alice as our example. Alice loves being fit and spends a lot of time researching how to be fitter, ways to help others get in shape, and what it would take to be a fitness trainer. Currently, Alice works as a financial consultant. But in her perfect life, she imagines waking up to a hearty, nutritious breakfast, which she shares with her partner. Then, she goes to the gym for a strength training session to start her day on a high note. She pictures a life where she can share her insights on social media platforms to educate more people and work with a few online clients at a time. In her perfect life, she goes out for lunch with her friends several times a week, has time for an afternoon nap, lives by the woods and takes a walk in nature every evening, prepares a home-cooked meal at the end of the day, and still has time to upload videos and meet with her clients.

CHAPTER 3: FINDING YOUR PERSONAL IKIGAI

And in this light, her vision board looks like this:

SEGMENT	VISION
Fitness and health	Nutritious breakfasts, Strength training, Home-cooked meals
Career (financial stability)	Health and fitness vlogs on social media A small, manageable online clientele
Social life (family and relationships)	Slow mornings with her partner Lunch with her friends
Mental health	Afternoon naps, Walks in nature Healthy relationships, Fulfillment in her career
Environment and Living Space	In nature, A cozy home
Work-life balance	A schedule that leaves time for all important things
Personal Development	Trying new healthy recipes, upskilling in the fitness niche
Leisure and Recreation	Brunches, traveling, hikes

In a vision board, Alice could visualize her life as follows:

It's simple, allows her to see what her life could be, and enables her to connect with what's important. Can you make a similar board for your life?

Once you have this, hang it in a spot where you can review it often. Each week, you will go through **Exercise 1**, assess the activities that align with what fulfills you, and choose what stays and what goes.

Have you narrowed down your interests? At this point, you may have about 3 to 5 top interests that seem core to your existence. Hold on to them as we are about to assess them further in line with your ikigai.

CHAPTER 3: FINDING YOUR PERSONAL IKIGAI

The Four-Circle Framework

"You have a masterpiece inside you, you know. One unlike any that has ever been created or ever will be. If you go to your grave without painting your masterpiece, it will not get painted. No one else can paint it. Only you."

- Gordon Mackenzie.

Remember the Ikigai picture I showed you in Chapter 1? It's now time to create our own. The final version will look like a more expounded illustration of the picture below. For now, I simply want you to take in the overall picture, noting the difference in what the circles entail – the next few steps will cover everything in more detail.

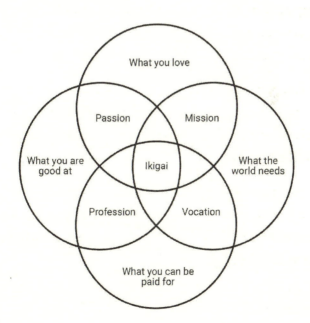

So, how do we get to your ikigai - that middle section where all the elements align? The idea in this section is to merge what you have learned about yourself in the previous section with what the world needs and what you can get paid for, which I will illustrate using an example. I will use Brian, a budding photographer with a passion for the community who has just turned 30 and is eager to set the tone for the rest of his life. Using his process as the guide, use this section as a practical exercise such that you fill out your framework as we go through each step. Ready? Let's get started.

Step 1: What do you love?

These are your passions and interests, which you will have figured out in **Section 1.** They can be hobbies, creative activities, or even things you love to discuss. For example, you can say that you love discussing sports and can go on and on about team strategies for hours.

Brian loves the following things:

- Helping others.
- Photography.
- Telling stories.
- Playing soccer.
- Rock balancing.

What about you? Can you list the interests you uncovered in the previous section?

CHAPTER 3: FINDING YOUR PERSONAL IKIGAI

HOBBIES	EXCITEMENT LEVEL	INTERESTS	EXCITEMENT LEVEL

Use **Exercise 1** from the previous section to help you cover this part. For example, you can have knitting as your hobby and Zumba as an interest.

Please note that by this point, you should have explored your interests, as explained in the previous section, so that you can gauge your excitement level and know how good you are at them. For example, you may be interested in learning how to make pasta but after a few classes, you may notice that your interest has waned despite your good progress. As such, you will know that if you were to make it the core of your ikigai, you would not feel fulfilled as this was a passing interest. So, which hobbies and interests have your full attention? These are the ones that go on the list.

Step 2: What are you good at?

Do you have any skills or talents that set you apart from other people? You can go back to **Exercise 4** in the previous section for insights on this, relying on what you know about yourself and what other people around you have noticed. We will focus on separating your skills into two. The first category is hard skills – specific skills you can learn by taking classes, e.g., data analysis. The second category is soft skills, which you adopt by working with other people and determine your ability to collaborate with others, e.g., communication.

In his research, Brian has found that he shines in the following aspects:

- He's very organized and loves analyzing data.
- He's a great communicator.
- He has excellent writing skills.
- He's resilient.

Note down your strengths and natural talents using the table below:

WHAT SOFT SKILLS ARE MY STRENGTHS?	HOW GOOD AM I ON A SCALE OF 1 TO 10?	WHAT HARD SKILLS ARE MY STRENGTHS?	HOW GOOD AM I ON A SCALE OF 1 TO 10?

These skills and talents should be things that you have tried and tested. For example, it's one thing to say that you are great at cooking. But it's another in entirety to make a meal from scratch, serve it to people, and get the same opinion.

Before you write down something as a skill or talent, ensure that you are objective and not basing your answers on your wishes. Have you truly proven that you have those skills or talents on your list? Also, have someone you trust rate your abilities on a scale or use an online assessment tool to gauge where you are. For example, if you think you are a good communicator, there are many online assessment tools that can put this to the test and rate you.

Step 3: What does the world need?

While it's possible for you to love and be good at something, it may not always fall into the larger ikigai picture. That's because to offer value to the world, your actions must positively affect the people around you. So, what can you do to address societal issues? Maybe you can tackle environmental issues, introduce changes in health, or simplify e-commerce. Whatever it is, it must consider the needs of the world or at least your community.

Having grown up in a food desert, Brian knows that his community needs the following things:

- More awareness about healthy foods.
- Access to healthy foods.
- Practical recipes for busy lifestyles.

What about your case? What gaps can you fill? Use the following table to write down areas where you can best serve the world.

WHAT DOES THE WORLD NEED?	WHY DOES IT NEED IT?	HOW SUSTAINABLE IS THIS NEED?

Now, how can you tell what the world needs? There are many sources of information. For example, Brian knows what his community needs as this is his lived experience. You can also source information from:

- **Engaging with the community** in person or through social media groups. People are constantly voicing their concerns; if you pay attention, you can land some gems.

- **Following updates on the media.** Please note that while news outlets are a great source of information, they can have some biases. As such, it's always best to follow up on anything you read, see, or hear by researching peer-reviewed articles and journals covering the same topics.

- **Reviewing surveys and reports.** Non-governmental organizations (NGOs), research organizations, and other reputable sources of information are always releasing findings about various industries you can rely on to discover emerging needs.

Also, look at your own life. Have you uncovered any need that you are unable to meet? Are other people facing the same problem? You can find out by engaging with your loved ones, posting surveys, or connecting with experts who may have answers to your questions. The information is out there if you put in the work to find it.

Step 4: What can you get paid for?

Many people need to make money from what they do as they require financial resources to support their lifestyles. Ikigai is a practical approach that takes this into account. So, once you have narrowed down possibilities in the first three steps, the last one looks into how you can monetize your passion. Examples include taking up a job, starting a business, or even going freelance. In this digital age, there are many ways to get compensated for offering value. What path will you choose?

Brian has his sights on the following options:

- **Start a blog on nutritional tips for people on a budget.** It provides value to people with busy lifestyles who need information on the go. He can use his photography and writing skills to make it appeal to more people.

- **Offer his photography and writing expertise to local NGOs** addressing societal health issues. He can enjoy a stable income while helping educate people on better eating habits to avoid lifestyle issues.

What of you? How many ways can you make money through your skills by offering value to the world while still tying what you do to your passions? Here is a table to help you with this:

QUESTION	ANSWER	BRIAN S EXAMPLE
What are my interests?		Helping others, telling stories, photography,
What are my current hard and soft skills?		Great communication, strong writing, and organization skills.
Which industries do my current skills and interests match?		Healthcare, social assistance, digital content creation, commercial photography, content marketing, freelance writing
Which of these industries have the most growth potential?		Social assistance, digital content creation, NGOs
Which career paths can I follow in these industries?		Creating a blog, digital content creation for NGOs, freelance writing
Which of these career paths aligns with my values?		NGOs as they offer community support and digital content creation to help people with tips.

Which of these career paths give me a work environment where I can thrive?		Photography for the chance to work with people, freelance writing for the freedom
Do I have experience in these career paths?		I've been working as a commercial photographer for two years and contributed to several blogs during this time.
Is there room for growth in these career paths?		Research shows that these industries will remain profitable for decades.

Answering these questions will help you narrow down your choices to figure out which paths are worth following. After all, you want to choose a path that fulfills you in all ways, and career stability is an important factor.

Explaining the Intersections

In finding your ikigai, you need to be aware of the relationships between each circle and how you can land on what will actually work. Here are the intersections to pay attention to:

Passion: The first intersection exists between **what you love and what you are good at**, as was the focus in the previous section. For example, Brian loves playing football but is not very good at it – even his loved ones have said as much. However, he is highly organized, which is essential for community work.

Moreover, he's great at writing, enabling him to share stories in ways that grab people's attention. As such, he'll focus on what he loves and is good or great at while putting the other items on the list to the side.

When you think of passion, don't think of it as just something you like doing. It must also relate to your strengths and weaknesses if it is to be part of your ikigai.

Mission: The second intersection looks at **what you love versus what the world needs**. For example, you may love reading the paper every morning as you sip on your coffee. But does the world really need this? Can it offer value to the community? Look at your interests and whether there are any ways you can spin them to be valuable to those around you. For example, Brian loves rock balancing as it helps him calm his mind. However, the world does not need this skill, so he cannot push it to the next stage of this process.

When it comes to those things you love but don't offer value to the world, I encourage you to hold onto them as hobbies—we should all have things that we enjoy just for ourselves. But as you find your ikigai, these will need to take a backseat.

Vocation: When you give the world value, it pays you back with value, which is often money. At this juncture, you want to compare **what the world needs versus what you can get paid for.** For example, we live in an age where climate action continues to pick up pace. As such, the world needs more environmentally sustainable solutions, and you can get paid for contributing to these; e.g., if you make energy-efficient electronics, you will contribute to an emerging need and get paid for it.

Profession. Now is the time to compare **what you are good at and what you can make money from**, which is another important intersection. In Brian's case, rock balancing is an art that calms him. But will anyone pay to see him balancing one rock on top of another? That's not likely, but in this social media age, you've probably seen someone get paid for much less. But viral social media videos aside, can you actually get paid for what you are good at? List all the items that can help you generate money and forget the others for now.

Reviewing Your Selections – Mistakes to Avoid

You've gotten this far – good job. But now, I will ask you to look at your list and ask yourself the following questions before we continue:

a. **Are the passions on your list truly things you would do if you were not getting paid?** Do you lose track of time when you are engaging in them? An interest does not equal a passion – interest fades, but passion remains even in the face of challenges.

b. **Are you being practical about your choices?** There are many things you can get paid for in this world. Trust me, I have come across some of the most unconventional careers. But does the world need what you are passionate about? Will it need it a year from now? How about five years from now? Financial viability is important.

c. **Are you sticking to only what you know?** In the quest for ikigai, you have to open yourself up to new ideas. When it comes to vocation and profession, look beyond what you know. Talk to other people in the field, use your networks, and remain open-minded. Had I closed myself off to what I knew, I would have stuck to writing investment books, yet my passion lay in philosophy. Are you avoiding what's unfamiliar out of fear or bias?

d. **Are you making assumptions?** My daughter once set up a lemonade stand outside our house because "it was sunny, and people buy lemonade when it's hot." The sales proved otherwise. Assuming that you know what people need can set you up for a disappointing journey. Rather than think you know what the world wants, take the time to conduct research and seek feedback from people you trust.

e. **Are you rushing through the process?** Each stage of this process is crucial in achieving your overall purpose. So, while you may be excited to find out what the rest of your life will look like, you should take the time to reflect on your answers. Use the exercises in the previous section to figure out your interests. Then, take the time to research the industry and match your skills with what the world needs.

f. **Are you expecting a definite answer?** Many people struggle with ikigai as they think there is one answer

CHAPTER 3: FINDING YOUR PERSONAL IKIGAI

for each person. But as you will later see, this process can result in various answers even in your case. What's more, your ikigai can change over time as you gain more insights into yourself. So, rather than seek one truth, be open to the fact that you may need to explore a few paths on your way to what works for you. It's a journey but a fulfilling one.

If you think you have made any of these errors in judgment, go back to the previous steps and redo the exercises. For example, you may have been narrowing all your choices so that you would have one profession instead of opening up to the possibility that you can excel in various areas. Have you made a similar mistake? Now is the best time to reflect on the reasons behind this and make a change.

Completing the Framework

With so many factors to consider, how do you choose your ikigai? It's a step-by-step process as follows:

a. **What are my passions?** Eliminate anything that does not fall into the passion intersection, i.e., the link between what you love and are good at.

b. **What are my missions?** Review what you love versus what the world needs. What stays on the list, and what remains a hobby or interest?

c. **What are my vocations and professions?** Look at the interconnectedness of what the world needs, what you can get paid for, and your interests. Here, you will use the question lists I used in steps 3 and 4 to check off options based on industry insights, your abilities, and interests.

Based on this, we can compile Brian's Ikigai as follows:

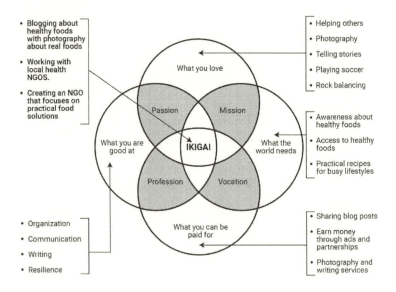

See? It's quite doable. By the end of this process, you will have a list of a few things you can do that will not only make you money but also provide value to the world and enable you to live in your purpose. How fun is that?

Your Reality Versus Your Ikigai

Suppose you have mapped your elements and found something that fits into the ikigai context. What now? Does this mean that you are about to embark on a complete overhaul of your life as you know it? Hardly. Let's use Debbie as our example. In

CHAPTER 3: FINDING YOUR PERSONAL IKIGAI

her framework, she's realized that she has a passion for doing makeup, is good at it, is always getting compliments on her face, has enough research that supports a career as a makeup artist, and knows that she can offer her services online through social media. What is her next step, and what should yours be?

a. **Be honest with yourself about your life as it is now.**

It's easy to jump at the first chance to change your life – you may even think of dropping everything to start your new life. But that's not the way to go about it. Instead, start by looking at your life right now.

- **What are your top priorities?** What aspects of your life hold the most weight and why? For example, Debbie has two children – she has to think of their needs as she embarks on a new path. As such, a sudden change in career might not work for her as it might for someone with fewer responsibilities.

- **What challenges might you face in pursuing your ikigai, and how will you deal with them?** What opportunities can you exploit? Think of everything from the resources available to you to any relationships that might get affected. For example, if Debbie wants to work as a makeup artist, she will need to take a course to refine her skills, which will mean more time away from her family. She has to think of ways to achieve a balance in this regard.

You need to work with what you have as you move towards where you want to be.

b. Start filling in the gaps.

We go back to our elements. In completing the framework, you always want to assess the viability of your choices as well as their practicality. How better is it to do this than by putting them to the test as follows?

- **Passions**. Make time for your top passions by integrating them into your daily routine. For example, in Debbie's case, if she were to pursue a career in makeup, this would be a daily thing. As such, she must carve out time to do makeup every day, whether this is ten minutes right before she dashes out to work or in the evening while she relaxes. The more you engage your passions, the more you can know if this is something you want to do in the long run - your experiences will be very telling.

- **Abilities**. Your strengths can always get better. Look at ways you can improve them, be it by practicing more or taking up classes. Chapter 4 will have more resources on how you can improve using kaizen techniques.

- **Value**. How can you start contributing more to the world? For example, Debbie knows that the world needs makeup services because people love feeling better about themselves. She can lean on this knowledge to start offering her services. What world need can you meet?

- **Financial wellbeing.** Finally, start looking for ways to make money through your passions. After all, you are offering value to the world and require financial resources to survive in this world. In Debbie's case, it's safe to say that she can start by advertising her services on social media while using her face as the canvas for what she can do.

It's all about setting the proper foundation so you can build solidly on it as you go.

c. **Be clear about your goals.**

Rome was not built in a day, nor will you achieve your ikigai in one stride. But you can lose heart if you look at how far you have left before you get to where you want to be. Here's how you can stay on track and still get satisfaction every step of the way:

- **Start with small goals.** Debbie knows that she wants to be a successful makeup artist who changes how people perceive themselves by making them feel more confident. But to get here, she has to do a few things, such as learning how to work on different faces, setting up her business, getting her first client, etc. Her efforts will be on these things as they will set her up for the future. What are your small goals? Write them down.

- **Connect with your overall vision.** What are you hoping to achieve? For example, Brian might be aiming at creating a blog that caters to thousands of people in food deserts, For instance, Brian may want to start a blog that serves thousands of people in areas that are considered food deserts (rural areas), helping them find affordable groceries possibly online, and teaching them how to make simple yet nutritious meals. Anytime he wants to know if he's making the right decision, he can look at how it affects this long-term vision.

What's your goal? Write it down. Better yet, use the visualization exercise from the previous section to connect with this concept.

d. Review, Adapt, Review – The Cycle Continues

Ikigai is not the final answer in your life. Instead, it is the key that unlocks a better life for you. So, you can expect changes to come your way along this journey. For example, while Debbie might think that launching an online business is the answer, she may find that she prefers teaching people how to do their makeup rather than doing it for them. Does this mean that she chose the wrong path? Hardly – it just means that she's got to tweak her approach a bit – she's still pursuing her passion, offering value to the world, and making money.

So, how can you approach such changes?

I. Conduct regular assessments (using exercise 1 in section 1). At first, you will need to do this every week, but over time, you can change it to once a month. But what are you looking for in these assessments?

- Are you happy with the direction you are heading? If not, what's not working, and what can you do about it?

- Have you noticed any new interests you would like to explore?

- Has your life changed in a way that affects your ability to pursue your ikigai?

The **exercises in the previous section** can help you reflect on your skills and interests as well as assess any new circumstances that may challenge you or provide new opportunities.

II. Open yourself up to change. Finding your ikigai might feel like you are finally home. So, the idea of changing anything can feel like a challenge. But remember what we said about complacency? Here is the thing – everything is subject to change. What you love will change. What the world needs will change. Your financial needs will change. Your skills will change. So, it's important to return to this framework every two to three months and ask yourself if you're keeping up with the changes. For example, if the world needs more people who offer versatile skills in your industry, that's a cue for you to commit to learning more things.

Do not stop learning just because you have found your ikigai. If anything, that should serve as the motivation to explore more interests.

e. **Celebrate your progress.**

Have you just finished a new course? Good job! Just got another client? Great! There will be many milestones in your journey, and it's important to remember to congratulate yourself each time you hit one. Treat your ikigai like a lifelong journey with many pit stops where you will deserve a pat on the back. For example, each time Brian's blog gets 100 new subscribers, he can gift himself with something he likes – that will give him the motivation to keep going.

CHAPTER 4:
Integrating Kaizen into Your Daily Routine

"We are what we repeatedly do. Excellence, then, is not an act but a habit."

- Aristotle.

When my brother-in-law lost his job due to regional company layoffs, he was distraught. But rather than wallow in what he could not control, he decided that he was finally going to embark on becoming a real estate agent. He'd always loved touring houses and could spend hours talking about dream houses. The job opportunity seemed like the perfect fit, and we all encouraged him to apply for it. But halfway through his first showing, he forgot everything about the house because his anxiety got the better of him. The second showing was also a disaster, with him blanking out on zoning laws, to the dismay of the would-be buyers. One bad experience after the other, he almost gave up on this dream. However, he'd always believed in bettering himself. So, he started shadowing better agents, learning from them, practicing his pitches on us and working on his anxiety. Now, he's so good at his job that he's toying with the idea of opening his own agency!

By acknowledging his shortcomings and working on them over time, my brother-in-law was undergoing continuous improvement. Does this remind you of something we covered in Chapter 2? It's all about kaizen, a practice that will help you level up your strengths so that you can offer more value to the world.

This practical chapter will walk you through the science of habit formation, how you can integrate changes in your life, and how to commit to self-improvement in the long term.

The Basics of Habit Formation

"Any act often repeated soon forms a habit, and habit allowed steady gains in strength. At first, it may be but as a spider's web, easily broken through, but if not resisted, it soon binds us with chains of steel."

- Tyron Edwards

Let's start with a simple exercise. Find a quiet spot where you can reflect on your behaviors for five to ten minutes with the aim of answering the following questions. Write down your answers at each step.

CHAPTER 4: INTEGRATING KAIZEN INTO YOUR DAILY ROUTINE

What bad habits do you have?

_____
_____
_____
_____

How have you cultivated them?

_____
_____
_____
_____

Can you think of how they started?

_____
_____
_____
_____

How long have you had them?

_____
_____
_____
_____

Answer these questions as honestly as you can. As we continue this chapter, you will get insights into why you have these habits and what it takes to build better ones.

For example, *I often stay up late past the right bedtime, even if it impacts my productivity the next day. I have been doing this for the last two months because I have been busy, and nighttime is the only time I have to focus on my hobbies, so I end up ignoring my bedtime to enjoy this me-time.*

What are your bad habits and why? Your answers at the start of this section will provide you with more insights into this.

The Cue-Routine-Reward Cycle.

Our habits do not form out of nothing – they are not innate to us. Instead, they result from a very interesting process we have all been through at several points in our lives. To illustrate this, I will use a common example – John has been trying to cut back on his snacking for years but cannot quite seem to stop. So, how did it all start, and how can this explain the habits in your life?

    a. **The cue or trigger**. Everyone has a trigger that pushes them to perform a habit. For example, every time John watches a movie, he reaches for a snack. As such, the cue is watching the movie.

What's your cue for your bad habits?

_____

_____

CHAPTER 4: INTEGRATING KAIZEN INTO YOUR DAILY ROUTINE

_____

_____

    b. **The behavior or routine.** A routine encompasses two things. The first is the cue, and the second is the action you take in response to the cue. In John's case, reaching for a snack when he puts a movie on encompasses the routine.

Can you find the routines in your case?

_____

_____

_____

_____

Examples: *Every time you open the fridge, you take a sip of wine. Every time you drive by a McDonald's, you grab a meal. Every time you are early to work, you stop by your friend's office.*

    c. **Reward.** What do you get from completing the routine? That is the benefit, aka reward, for the habit. Whatever you get from the habit releases dopamine in your system, signaling that the habit has positive benefits, be it pleasure or relief. (I mentioned this under procrastination in Chapter 2, and you can refer to that chapter for more context.) John, for instance, gets pleasure from eating snacks.

How do you feel each time you engage in your bad habits? Write down the rewards below.

_____

_____

_____

_____

We can look at the habit cycle in the following way:

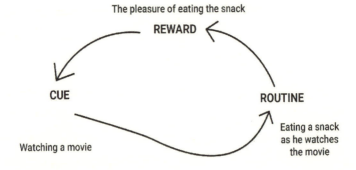

d. Repetition. Doing something once or a few times does not a habit make. Instead, habits take time to form, going through the motions of cue, routine, and reward. But how long does it take for the habit to stick?

Lally et al. (2010) found that the habit formation period ranges from 18 to 254 days, which depends on the complexity of the behavior, how consistent you are, whether your environment has cues that support the behavior, and a hoard of psychological factors, e.g., your motivation. So, each time you repeat a behavior, you take one step closer to forming a habit. Behaviors like drinking water are easy to turn into habits as they are easy to accomplish. But when it comes to complex routines like working out, most people need time to turn these into habits.

e. **Craving.** Repeat a behavior enough times, and your brain gets accustomed to the rewards. Soon enough, it starts pushing you to repeat the behavior so you can experience the pleasure or relief you get from the behavior. Eventually, this repetition becomes automatic as your anticipation for the reward can become so powerful that it overpowers your other senses.

See the cycle? Let's look at how it all began for John. One day, he was watching a movie and decided to have a snack. He loved it. Consequently, the next time he wanted to watch a movie, he grabbed another snack because he could relate the experience with pleasure. Slowly but surely, this became his routine, such that anytime he thinks of watching a movie, he can already picture the snack he will have. What's more, he finds himself watching more movies, which allows him to enjoy more snacks. It's become ingrained in his reward system.

Our diagram thus changes to encompass the craving as follows:

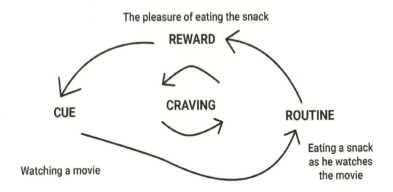

Can you see how easy it is for our brains to register habits? Think about the following things:

- Brushing your teeth in the morning.
- Turning off the lights before going to bed.
- Taking a shower after coming home.
- Washing your hands after using the washroom.
- Moisturizing your face after bathing.

How often do you have to think about these routines? How do you feel each time you complete them? How long have you been doing them?

For most people, these activities feel like second nature, things that come so naturally to them that they don't need to add them to a to-do list. But they are not – they are habits that you have ingrained in yourself for so long that they have become a part of who you are.

With habit creation being so subtle, it's easy to see why many people have bad habits that they cannot seem to kick. But that's also the beauty of this process. In the same way you can adopt bad habits, you can also incorporate better ones into your life to align with your purpose and give you more satisfaction.

Can You Change Your Life in Just 21 Days? The Science of Repetition.

This book's title hinges on mastering Japanese wisdom in 21 days. But does this mean that you will outgrow all your bad habits in this time? Not at all. As stated in the habit creation cycle, habits form within 18 to 254 days, depending on factors such as complexity, your environment, how consistent you are, and how committed you are to your goals. Some habits may kick in within the 21-day window. However, for most of the habits that will be essential to accomplishing your ikigai, this 21-day period will serve as the foundation on which you will establish new habits and break out of the bad ones. So, what does this mean? Well, for you to succeed in this journey, you will have to be **consistent** with the good habits you will choose.

Why? Repetition is a key component in any habit-creation cycle. For example, if you want to protect your skin from harmful rays from the sun, you will wear sunscreen. Do this on the first day, and you'll be proud of yourself. Do it again on day two, and you'll be happy with your progress. But what happens if you skip day three? You'll likely be discouraged. How about if you skip day four? You might start thinking that sunscreen application is too much of a task. Eventually, you will likely give up on the idea. But what if you were to apply sunscreen no matter what? You'd find that it would soon become a part of your life that you just embarked on without thinking about – that's the power of consistency.

To sum it up, consistency (repeating a behavior) comes with the perks below:

- It makes the **routine feel natural** by strengthening the neural pathways in your brain to become accustomed to the activity.

- It **gives you the push you need** to integrate an activity into your life. The first few times might feel challenging, but the resistance to change will decrease over time.

- It **creates a routine** in which your brain knows what to expect and when, which creates a familiarity that cements the behavior.

- It **helps you track your progress**, prompting you to be more accountable as you can tell how well you are doing.

- It **boosts your dopamine levels** as you feel accomplished each time you stick to the routine.

- It **strengthens your willpower** such that you pay less attention to distractions.

CHAPTER 4: INTEGRATING KAIZEN INTO YOUR DAILY ROUTINE

Best of all, consistency helps you build the habits you want in the long run. For example, suppose you want to start eating more vegetables. In that case, you can create a meal plan that includes one serving of vegetables a day. Each time you tick off a meal with vegetables, you will feel a rush of **dopamine** because of the joy of following through with the commitment, which will encourage you to keep sticking to the plan. And as you continue tracking your progress, you will hardly notice how much eating vegetables has become a part of you. One day, you'll wake up and be that person who orders a salad in a restaurant!

Beware of the Intensity Trap: Choose Micro Habits Instead

Do you know why most people fail at building better habits? It's not that they are not aware of their bad habits, nor is it because they do not want to be better. Instead, it comes down to how they approach the habit changes – they choose to go big or go home. Someone who has been sedentary for the last year suddenly wants to be at the gym for three hours every day. A person who barely works five hours a day now wants to start pulling ten hours each day.

While such goals are admirable, they are often unsustainable in the long run – most people realize that they began with impossible routines and abandon the behavior change altogether. It's pretty much what we see every New Year – big resolutions in January that turn into memories as each month passes.

What's the alternative to high intensity? The goal of changing your bad habits or embracing better ones lies in setting small goals and being **consistent** about them. Not only does this help you build momentum, but it also protects you from burnout, helps you reinforce your neural pathways gradually, is better for creating a routine, and gives you the progress you need to boost your self-discipline.

So, what does this look like? Say, for example, you spend three hours (180 minutes) a day on social media just scrolling your phone. Your main goal might be reducing this time to just 20 minutes daily. But remember, you have cues that trigger you to scroll, be it boredom, curiosity, or procrastination. These cues won't just go away because you have decided to spend less time online. So, instead of going for 20 minutes at once, you will start with a smaller goal, such as reducing your scrolling time by 20 minutes each week. Starting at 180 minutes, you'd go down to 160, 140, 120, 100, 80, 60, 40, and then 20. That would take a total of 8 weeks, allowing you to find the transition easy while giving you time to figure out better ways to spend the extra time you will save.

Success in life comes down to mastering the basics and relying on them to achieve the bigger things. That's the focus of this chapter and the overall book – kaizen all the way. Now, let's get practical with some exercises:

Replacing Unhelpful Habits

We are now back to the answers you wrote down as we started this chapter. What are your bad habits, and how have they affected you? What are the cues? Which of these habits is holding you back from pursuing your ikigai? The whole point of this Chapter is to weed out behaviors that curtail you while building those that help you. For example, assume you've decided to pursue your passion for organic farming and turn this into a business, but you are easily distracted. In such a case, you'd need to address your distractions to focus on the goal in front of you.

So, based on your ikigai, what habits need to go? Here is how you can get to the bottom of these setbacks and turn things around:

Exercise 1: Recognizing Your Triggers.

Habit formation and the overall habit cycle must have a trigger – the cue that prompts you to respond by engaging in a routine. We will use Kevin as our example. He's working on pursuing his ikigai as an organic farmer, which requires him to be on the farm in the morning. But each time the alarm goes off, he hits the snooze button. The reward is the extra five minutes of sleep. But he has noticed that snoozing not only makes him more tired but also makes it harder for him to be out of the house in time. Something so simple profoundly impacts his life, but he can't seem to snap out of it.

So, how can you find the triggers for your bad habits? The following exercise, which I based on Kevin's example, shows you how to go about it.

Step 1: Keep a habit journal where you write down the bad habits you have engaged in throughout the day. Fill this out every evening as you reflect on your day. Example: Today, I hit the snooze button five times.

Step 2: Connect with your physical and emotional states. How were you feeling right before you engaged in the habit? What factors may have played into your actions? These can be emotional or physical. Example: I was feeling extremely tired in the morning and hit the snooze button to get more sleep.

Step 3: Look at when you often indulge in your habits. Are there patterns? E.g., you may find that you often snooze your alarm on Mondays because you sleep late on Sundays.

Step 4: Analyze your habits and look for any common patterns using the if-then technique. For example, you may find that you always hit the snooze button if you've slept late the night before. So, **if** you sleep late, **then** you feel too tired to stick to your alarm routine.

In a table, your habit journal will look like this.

HABIT	HOW WAS I FEELING EMOTIONALLY? WHY?	WHAT WAS MY PHYSICAL STATE? WHY?	WHAT TIME WAS IT?	WHAT DAY WAS IT?
I hit the snooze button five times.	I was overwhelmed by how little I had slept.	I was too tired to get up as I had slept at 1 am.	6 am	Monday

Fill it out with your own bad habits and keep at it for a week. Over time, you'll start noticing that there is a relationship between your bad habits and your emotional and physical state. For example, you may find that you turn on the TV whenever you have a lot of work to do. So, your statement will look like this: **if** I have too much work on my plate, **then** I watch TV to distract myself.

Exercise 2: Substituting Your Bad Behaviors

Exercise 1 will help you recognize the triggers in your habit cycles, which will be important in re-engineering the cue-behavior-reward cycle into the reminder-behavior-reward cycle. How?

Step 1: Assess the needs that you have been trying to fulfill with your bad habits. Exercise 1 groups these into physical and emotional needs – you can be seeking relief (e.g., by procrastination), comfort (e.g., by eating junk foods at night), or pleasure (e.g., by watching cartoons) – figure out what you are looking for by looking at the patterns.

In Kevin's case, his need is physical such that he hits the snooze button to get a few extra minutes of sleep.

Step 2: Find a way to meet that need without reinforcing the bad habit. Say, for example, that you often reach for a soda whenever you feel stressed, but this has been affecting your health. Think of other ways you can get stress relief, e.g., taking a walk, talking to a friend, etc.

In Kevin's case, he believes that he needs at least seven hours of sleep.

Step 3: Work with a plan. The best way to work through a bad habit is to create a plan, as this emphasizes consistency. For example, Kevin can choose to sleep by 11 pm every night. To stick to this, he will set an alarm for 10.50 pm that reminds him to be in bed by 11 pm. Section 2 will show you how to come up with a plan.

Step 4: Stick to the plan. A daily routine is the most effective way of maintaining consistency. So, whatever you choose to do to replace the bad habits, keep doing it until it feels like second nature.

It's important to note that bad habits have a way of creeping up again over time. You will need to monitor your activities to check if this is happening so you can stick to or adjust your plan accordingly.

Small Steps for Big Changes

"Don't try to rush progress. Remember—a step forward, no matter how small, is a step in the right direction. Keep believing."

- KARA GOUCHER.

My friend is a finance coach who helps people master how to make the most out of their income. You'd think that he starts by getting them to draw balance sheets, map out long-term strategies, or even start side hustles. But it's not even close. He gets them on the right track by asking them to track just one expense

CHAPTER 4: INTEGRATING KAIZEN INTO YOUR DAILY ROUTINE

every day. At first, his clients think it's a joke and wonder how this will help them be financially wise. Eventually, the ability to keep track of just one expense a day starts making sense to them because they later get to two and then three, and by the end of it, they can actually account for every expense they have. But if he were to ask them to start by tracking all their expenses, he'd overwhelm them, which is the last thing they need.

Micro habits are smaller components of your goal habits that you can easily achieve, which makes them the perfect way to work towards any goal. Here are some examples.

- Instead of aiming for eight glasses of water a day, aim for one glass in the morning.

- Instead of shooting for reading an entire book, go through one page every evening.

- Instead of joining the gym, do ten squats every day.

Think of the smallest building block of the habit you want to embrace and work on that. It will feel easy, will not overwhelm you, will enable you to build momentum, and will allow you to work on your self-discipline so that you can stick to your plan. Best of all, it's easy to implement.

Exercise 1: Creating Your Micro Habits

In any habit you embrace, you must think of the overall goal in the future. We will use two people. The first is Kevin, our alarm snoozer, as our example. He wants to get up at 6 am every day without hitting the snooze button. The second is Troy, whose doctor has advised him to start drinking more water to address his current health issues. So, how can our examples set the goals that will determine their habits?

    a. Specificity: A goal must be clear on what you want to accomplish, when, and where. Example: Kevin wants to wake up at 6 am every day, even on weekends. What's your specific goal? Troy wants to drink at least eight glasses of water every day and cut back on sodas.

    b. Measurability: How will you track your goal? For example, when you are losing weight, you can say that you want to lose 10 pounds. In Kevin's case, the measure will be waking up at 6 am seven days a week. In Troy's case, the measure is the number of glasses of water per day.

    c. Achievability: How will you achieve the goal? Kevin may want to start waking up at 6 am every day. But since he hasn't been doing so for a while, he must be realistic about his progress. So, his goal can look like "I want to start waking up at 6 am two days a week. Then I will increase this to three times, four times…. until I can cover the whole week." Troy, who has been hydrating with sodas, cannot go cold turkey and expect success. His goal can look like, "I want to start drinking one glass of water a day for the first week. Then I will move on to two glasses the next week and three the week after that until I can hit eight glasses of water a day in eight weeks."

CHAPTER 4: INTEGRATING KAIZEN INTO YOUR DAILY ROUTINE

Here is where we get the **micro habits**.

So, when and how should you scale your micro habits? It comes down to how well you have stuck to the original targets, how ready you are to take on the next step, and how easy you find the current goal. If you pass these three checks, you can scale up, ensuring you are neither complacent nor pushing yourself too much.

d. **Relevance**: How does your goal tie to your ikigai? Remember that the point of this book is to achieve your purpose. In Kevin's case, he wants to be more productive at his work, which requires him to show up early and be energetic. In Troy's case, he wants to enjoy better health, as without it, he cannot pursue his passion optimally.

e. **Timeliness**: When is the deadline? You must have a way to gauge your progress. For example, Kevin may decide that he wants to be waking up at 6 am every day within the next six weeks. Troy wants to get to eight glasses of water a day in eight weeks.

Using the same criteria, lay out your goals in this table, using Kevin's and Troy's examples:

CRITERIA	KEVIN'S EXAMPLE	TROY'S EXAMPLE	YOUR GOAL
Specificity	To wake up on time so I can show up early to work.	To drink enough water to hydrate my body.	
Measurability	To wake up by 6 am. I will track this using my alarm.	To drink eight glasses of water. I will track the number of glasses.	
Achievability	To wake up by 6 am. every day of the week. I plan to start by waking up at 6 am two days a week and then increasing this regularity.	To drink eight glasses of water a day. I will start by drinking one glass in the first week before building on this to hit eight glasses.	
Relevance	To be less tired and more productive at my work.	To hydrate my body better and cut back on my soda reliance.	
Timeliness	To wake up at 6 am. every day within the next six weeks.	To be drinking eight glasses of water a day within the next eight weeks.	
Overall statement	I want to wake up at 6 am every day to create a sleep routine that helps me show up at my best.	I want to be drinking eight glasses of water a day as this will help me cut back on sodas and improve my overall health.	

CHAPTER 4: INTEGRATING KAIZEN INTO YOUR DAILY ROUTINE

Using your goals, find the micro habits that are necessary to achieve them. For example, Kevin will need to wake up at 6 am twice in the first week. Then, three times on the second week, four on the third, five on the fourth, six on the fifth, and seven on the sixth week. That's achievable progress as it allows him to build on what he's done the previous week.

What's on your table? Can you find the micro habits that can get you there? Write them down below:

_____

_____

_____

_____

Exercise 2: The Reminder-Routine-Reward Cycle

Remember how we form habits? We will rely on the same principles to help you nurture your micro habits, as follows:

I. **Choose a cue.** Every habit needs a cue. For example, if Kevin wants to wake up every morning at 6 am, he will set an alarm for 6 am. If you want to work out first thing in the morning, you will lay out your gym clothes by the bed before you sleep. The sound of the alarm or the sight of the clothes will remind you of what you need to do. What's yours?

_____

_____

II. **Address possible challenges.** It's easy to know what you need to do and still choose not to follow through. For example, Kevin might hear his alarm and turn it off or snooze it. To avoid this, he can place his alarm several feet away from his bed, forcing him to get out of bed. What about you? What challenges might you face, and how can you address them?

III. **Create a sound environment.** Your environment plays a crucial role in how well you adopt new habits. For example, if Kevin wants to wake up well-rested, he must make sure he sleeps well and on time – this may require him to turn off the lights, lay off smart devices before sleeping, and invest in comfortable bedding.

What can you do to improve your chances of enjoying the small changes in your life?

CHAPTER 4: INTEGRATING KAIZEN INTO YOUR DAILY ROUTINE

IV. **Include rewards.** You'll remember that the dopamine system responds to how we feel after we complete a routine. How better to appeal to it than to gift yourself for sticking to the plan? For example, each time Kevin gets up at 6 am., he can spend some time thanking himself for sticking to his promise. What's more, at the end of each week or month, reward yourself if you have met your goals.

Over time, you will find that the micro habits are much easier to accomplish, paving the way for them to be a part of your life.

Exercise 3: Tracking Your Micro Habits

There are many ways to track your progress but I will keep it simple yet effective using the table below. Let's use Kevin, our budding organic farmer, as our example again. He wants to stop hitting the snooze button and to get up at 6 am. So, the micro habit is to get up at 6 am.. The goal in the first week is to get up twice at 6 am for a reward of a new watch. He's achieved his goal and thus marked it as 2/2. Use the same table to write down your habits and track your progress, checking off what you have completed.

	KEVIN'S EXAMPLE		GOAL 1		GOAL 2	
Habit	Wake up at 6 am.					
Goal	2 times					
Progress	2/2	√				
Reward	Watch	√				

Then, using the tracker below, you can gauge how well your micro habits are progressing in relation to your overall goal. Each time you accomplish a goal, you tick it off in the calendar using a (√), and then you check your progress at the end of each week and each month per your target.

Let's use Kevin's example to show how progress is tracked in operation.

WEEK NUMBER	MONDAY	TUESDAY	WEDNES-DAY	THURS-DAY	FRIDAY	SATUR-DAY	SUNDAY
1		√		√			
2		√		√	√		
3		√	√		√	√	
4		√	√	√		√	√
5	√		√	√	√	√	√

In five weeks, he's managed to go from hitting his snooze button to waking up at 6 am. And as he heads into the sixth week, he only has to hit waking up at 6 am. all days of the week and he will be good to go. I will include a similar template in the final worksheets to help you track your progress in this way.

SMALL STEPS LEAD TO BIG RESULTS!

By now, you've explored the power of **small, daily improvements** through Kaizen and the importance of aligning your life with Ikigai. **But are you taking action?**

Make your progress tangible with the **Ikigai & Kaizen Workbook**—designed to guide you through **daily habit tracking, goal-setting, and purpose discovery.**

Scan the QR code now or follow the link to access your **printable worksheets** and start implementing these life-changing practices today!

https://personalgrowthpages.com/winston-ikigai-workbook

CHAPTER 5:
Balancing Work and Personal Life with Ikigai

"Don't get so busy making a living that you forget to make a life."

- DOLLY PARTON.

Have you ever listened to "9 to 5" by Dolly Parton? The lyrics encompass the working experience for most people. At some point, she states, *"It's a rich man's game, No matter what they call it, And you spend your life Puttin' money in his wallet."* From the time this song was released to date, it has always resonated with people who work for others. After all, many of them are working for the money, as I mentioned in Chapter 3, and they find no joy in what they are doing. So, every day they put in feels like a challenge, chasing after someone else's dream, resulting in feelings of discontentment and frustration.

And then there's you – Now that you have found your ikigai, you are safe, right? Not quite. While you will find joy in your work, you might find yourself singing a very different tune – one that talks about how little time you have left for other aspects of your life, including your loved ones. I've seen many people throw themselves at their jobs or businesses out of passion and succeed but have little to show for other aspects of their lives. So, where is the balance, and how can you achieve it?

Harmonizing Passion and Profession

"Follow your passion. Nothing—not wealth, success, accolades, or fame—is worth spending a lifetime doing things you don't enjoy."

- JONATHAN SACKS.

Mark, a senior writer at a magazine, loves his job. It pays him well enough to cater to his family and gives him the security he needs to plan for the future. However, in seeking his ikigai, he has realized that he has a passion for reviewing tech gadgets, is good at it, and that there is a whole market for this. But he does not want to quit his writing career. So, how can he blend the two?

Chapter 3 covers how to find your ikigai. Many people will throw themselves into pursuing this as their sole career or business. But what of people who want to balance what they are currently doing with their passions? Here's how you can do this while still showing up 100% at work:

Keep it as a hobby. A passion is something you love doing such that you pursue it even without getting paid for it. Make your passion a priority in your life so that you have a routine that

CHAPTER 5: BALANCING WORK AND PERSONAL LIFE WITH IKIGAI

encompasses it. For example, Mark can carve out one hour each day to work on his gadget reviews. He still gets to show up at work but gets this time where he's doing something just for him.

Integrate your passion with your job. Are there aspects of your passion that spill over to what you do? For example, Mark is a senior writer. He can talk to his editor about writing more tech gadget reviews, enabling him to work on projects that align with his passion. Look for projects in your business or job that align with your interests or create opportunities for the same. For example, even if the magazine may not have tech content, Mark can suggest writing guest post articles on the blog.

Turn it into a side hustle. While passions are not always money-oriented, it's always good to have some extra money coming into your account. So, what skills or services can you offer that relate to your passion? In Mark's case, he can set up a blog or a vlog to share his reviews, and he can earn money from ads or brand partnerships. Suppose you love making craft beer. You can bottle it and sell it at a profit. How can you have fun and still make money? Think about this and write it down.

Share your passion with the world for free. Since passion and money are not glued at the hip, you can use your talents to improve your community, as many people in Okinawa do. How? Look at community projects or NGOs where your services can come in handy. For example, if you love photography and an NGO is advocating for environmental conservation, you can help them cover this segment with a photo shoot. In Mark's case, he can teach underprivileged kids how to use tech to better their lives, giving them a leg up in the world. How can you create value while enjoying your passion?

You can also choose to do a combination of these. For example, Mark can choose to start a vlog on tech gadgets while still working on local community projects. In fact, he can do all four by keeping his reviews as a hobby he shares through his vlog, which the community can access for free, allowing him to earn money from ads and partnerships. See? There are many ways to align your passion with your career or business, but balance is important, as we will cover in this section.

Using 'Flow' State for Optimal Productivity

Have you ever been so engrossed in a task that nothing else mattered, and all your focus was on it? Have you ever lost track of time because you were enjoying a task so much that you barely kept up with the passing of the hours? That's called "flow state," which people also refer to as "being in the zone."

It's a mental state where everything around you disappears (loss of self-consciousness), and you focus on doing what's in front of you (intense focus), immersing all your senses in the process (loss of track of time) and caring only about what you are doing (emphasis on excellence). But while you may not have an awareness of time, you maintain control over the task, enjoying every bit of progress you make in it as this motivates you to keep going.

Being in the zone does not hinge on the goal but rather on the work that it takes to get there. For example, Mark, our tech gadget reviewer, might find that he feels this way anytime he's working on a script for his latest review. Everything else fades away as he zeroes in on what he will include, filtering what's necessary, looking at what keywords will rank best, and coming up with the overall version. While the goal is to have an excellent review in the end, that takes a backseat as he focuses on every bit that will culminate in the final vlog.

Being in the "flow state" comes with many advantages. For one, you are not distracted, which allows you to be keener on what you are doing, paving the way for more creativity and productivity. Secondly, it challenges you so that you learn more about each task and your abilities. Most importantly, it gives you more satisfaction from your tasks. After all, what can be more rewarding than engaging in your passion and reviewing the progress at each stage?

However, there is such a thing as overdoing things, even your passion. For example, Mark loves talking about new gadgets. So, as he pursues his passion for sharing his views, he may spend hours on end on his videos, neglecting his other responsibilities, including his main job and his family. But if he focuses too much on his family and job, he will find that he's losing momentum with his videos, which will result in dissatisfaction. The only way to have your cake and eat it is to seek balance, such that you can get in and out of the zone per a set routine.

But how do you get here?

Choose a SMART (specific, measurable, achievable, relevant, and timed) goal for the session. It's difficult to remain focused when the task is too simplistic or too challenging – that's when you start looking for distractions. Strike a balance between the two to challenge yourself without feeling overwhelmed. For example, Mark can choose to work on one 10-minute vlog within two hours.

Prioritize the tasks. What must you do to reach your goal? Say, for example, that you want to bake some lasagna. You'd start by prepping the ingredients before baking the dish. What are your prep activities? Figure out what you need to do and when you need to do them to ensure you remain in that flow state.

Get rid of distractions. You can't get into "the zone" when you are on your phone, talking to someone, or distracted by anything else. Choose a spot where you can focus on the task at hand, ensuring you have everything you need – snacks, water, etc. It's also best to start with a bathroom break to avoid discomfort or frequent breaks.

Focus on the building blocks rather than the goal. What processes must you complete to achieve your goal? Focus on those instead of the outcome to ensure you remain in the present. For example, if you are trying to write a story, don't dwell on the ending. Instead, focus on the plot – the rest will fall into place.

Finally, take a break as needed. Chapter 6 has more on how you can manage your time better to ensure productivity without overwhelming yourself.

CHAPTER 5: BALANCING WORK AND PERSONAL LIFE WITH IKIGAI

Creating Boundaries between Work and Life

"Almost everything will work if you unplug it for a few minutes…including you."

- ANNE LAMOTT.

When I worked in investment, I met many interesting people, but few came close to Nathan, whose name I changed for privacy reasons. Nathan was the kind of guy whose achievements I hoped to have someday. He was always well-groomed, walked with quiet confidence, knew what he was doing, and brought in the top investors in the company – his rise to partner was not a surprise to anyone. But here's the thing - Nathan was not working himself to the ground like the rest of us. He'd show up at almost ten in the morning, have a few meetings, and leave for a long lunch at one in the afternoon. The next time we'd see him was at about three in the afternoon, and by six in the evening, he was out the door when most of us had at least three more hours of work – he barely even came in on Fridays.

Somehow, he had found a way to excel without compromising his well-being. Back then, it seemed impossible. But knowing what I know now, Nathan's way of life was not a unicorn. He was a man who chose to create a work-life balance that enabled him to show up as his best, not just in our company but also as a friend and a family man. Whatever time he gave, he was always fully present, and that made all the difference.

There are many Nathans in Okinawa and the world, and here's the recipe to their success and how you can also strike that delicate balance:

The Art of Saying No.

Nathan was not a rude man. But many people did not go to him for help or advice unless it was necessary – we all respected his time. The reason? – He had no problem saying "no" to things that did not serve his purpose at work. It might seem like an easy thing, but many people have a hard time saying "no" to others because they are afraid of other people's perceptions. But if you accept almost every other proposal that lands on your desk, not only do you tire yourself out, but you also create an environment where people may push their work on you just because they know you will accept it, yet they can actually do it by themselves.

The key to knowing what you can take on lies in knowing your abilities, your current workload, what tasks are most important to you, how much time you have, and the capacity you have to take on any other tasks. Let's use the example of Eric. He's representing a client in court in the next two hours and needs to finalize his prep. A colleague comes in, asking for advice on something that will take an hour of Eric's time. However, it's an issue that can wait till after Eric is in court. "No" is the answer that will best serve Eric. But blurting out a "no" is not the way to go about it.

If you are ever in a situation where you cannot help others but want to let them down gently yet assertively, here's how you can go about it:

Be straightforward. You want to be polite about your inability to help the other person without leaving any room for ambiguity; otherwise, you can give the other person false hope, which can result in a misunderstanding. For example, Eric can say, "I am sorry. I can't help you with this right now. I'm prepping for a court hearing that's in two hours."

Be honest about your reason. There are many reasons why you may be unable to help a colleague or client. You may not have the skills, may lack time, may have too much on your plate, etc. Briefly state the reason as this communicates why you are not the best person for the job, e.g., "I am on my lunch break and won't be back till 2 pm." There's no need to go into too many details, as a summary should be enough.

Propose other solutions. Sometimes, you cannot help someone when they initially make a request but have the ability to help them later. Or you may know someone who can help them. For example, Eric may have another colleague, Martha, who can help his colleague. He can say, "Martha is well-versed in this and might be available to help." Or he can say, "I will be out of court in the next three hours. I can help you then." Solutions are a polite way of offering someone help without taking on too much work. But even with these, you must ensure you are not giving someone false hope or agreeing to something that will put too much pressure on you.

Be empathetic. Saying "no" requires you to also consider the other person's position. It takes a lot to ask for help. As such, acknowledge that you are grateful that this person thought of asking you for help and let them know that you understand the importance of their request. But even as you do this, stand firm in your decision to say no. Some people may try to push you to see if you can offer leeway, while others may try to manipulate you emotionally, if you say no. It's important to empathize with them and remain polite without allowing their feelings to sway where you stand.

If you have been putting other people's needs first for a long time or care a lot about what other people have to say about you, it will take a while before you master this art. But when faced with a challenge, remember that a "no" to others is a "yes" to yourself. And you need as many of those "yeses" as you can get in your quest for balance.

Designing a Work-Life Framework.

Managing investors' accounts was not easy. In fact, many of us were in a constant state of physical, emotional, and mental exhaustion, relying on caffeine to keep us barely awake. Yet Nathan, who was bringing in the top clients and had a lot to lose if he slipped up, always looked like he was getting enough sleep, sunshine, water, you name it. But it's not that he was not working hard – he was; he was just doing it in a better way that allowed him to prioritize his well-being just as he maximized his productivity.

Not everyone can show up at work at 10 am and take a two to three-hour lunch break. But that does not mean that you cannot design a framework that works to benefit you personally and professionally. Here are simple ways to perfect that work-life balance:

Create a set routine. Say you work in a company – you know what hours you must be at work. Use that to create a routine, e.g., you clock in at 8 am and leave at 4 pm. These are work hours – at this time, you focus on being productive and meeting your goals. Then, you can schedule time for your loved ones, e.g., hang out with your friends or meet with other people till 7 pm, go home and be with family till 10 pm, work on your passion for an hour, and be in bed by midnight. Even if you are a remote worker, you can use the same concept to create a balance. So, what works for you and why? Write it down.

Have clear boundaries. These work at home and at work. For example, if your kids love calling you while you are at work, make it clear that they can only do so if it is urgent. If not, they can wait till you are on break or at home. The same goes for your work. Unless you have a job that requires you to be on the clock at all times, you should have boundaries between you and your job. For example, if you clock out at 5 pm, your colleagues should know not to expect you to answer calls or emails until you clock in the next day. Even if you work from home, these personal and professional boundaries must be in place.

Take personal time. At the end of the day, you are an individual whose needs transcend personal and work responsibilities. The next chapter will show you how to cater to these. But for you to give this your all, you must have time for yourself in your routine, e.g., every day, I will take an hour to catch up on my favorite TV show.

Creating a routine is actually the easy part – sticking to it is what becomes a challenge. But by weeding out unhelpful habits, such as people-pleasing, you can actualize what other people may find elusive. As we cover the next chapters, you will learn more about how you can perfect a routine that aligns with your passion, work, and all other aspects of your life.

CHAPTER 6:
Practical Kaizen Strategies for Every Aspect of Life

"Little by little, one travels far."

- J.R.R. Tolkien.

How often have you come across someone who excels in one area of life but faces challenges in almost every other area of their life? Many people face this problem. I'll give you the example of Simon, a man I met when I was still knee-deep in the rat race. He was a jeweler who made such beautiful pieces that he always had orders coming in – people could not get enough of his work. And he never disappointed them, always ensuring that each of his pieces was a work of art. But while he was a genius in this regard, Simon barely took care of himself. Not only did he appear disheveled most times, but he also did not clean up after himself, despite working from his loft and forcing his clients to put up with many awkward situations.

Working long hours, Simon barely ate nutritious food, got much sunlight, interacted with people other than his clients, or had any hobbies. His focus was on his passion and nothing else. Eventually, his health took a turn for the worse. Doctors tried to get to the root of the problem, but the truth was that Simon's issues stemmed from a poor lifestyle – the only way out was by taking a break, something that did not go down well with him. He had to choose between survival and pursuing what he loved – you can imagine just how hard that was.

While you may not be neglecting yourself to the point of hospitalization, you may be compromising in some areas of your life. But like I emphasized in Chapter 2, your life is multidimensional, such that if you neglect one area of your life, this spills over to other aspects of your well-being, ultimately affecting your ability to lead a fulfilling life. This Chapter shows you how you can make small improvements that will have significant impacts on all aspects of your life.

Kaizen for Personal Development

"Success is nothing more than a few simple disciplines, practiced every day."

- Jim Rohn.

Studies have shown that routines are essential in our personal and work lives as they help us establish good habits and boost our self-discipline, as explained in Chapter 4. But that's not all they do – they also eliminate decision fatigue and help you

CHAPTER 6: PRACTICAL KAIZEN STRATEGIES FOR EVERY ASPECT OF LIFE

remain focused, which makes you more productive. Take the example of Dwayne "The Rock" Johnson. He gets up at 4 am, starts his day with a workout, eats a healthy breakfast, and then spends the rest of his day working on projects while incorporating family time. And by 8 pm, he's in bed, ready to get enough rest so he can do it all over again the next day. So, what does he get out of this? Professionally, he's managed to maintain a physique that continues to open doors for him in Hollywood, and his routine allows him to show up optimally at work. And in his personal life, he gets to invest in his overall health and enjoy enough family time. So, he's not just excelling in one thing and falling short in other areas.

Let's look at Jeff Bezos' routine. How do you think the Amazon founder spends his time? Well, it may surprise you to know that he doesn't actually use an alarm clock to wake up and instead relies on his natural circadian rhythm, ensuring he gets at least eight hours of sleep. Once up, he takes his time to enjoy a slow morning as he reads the paper and connects with his family. His meetings typically start at around 10 am., and by afternoon, he's cleared his calendar to focus on decision-making and other tasks. Come evening, he heads home to spend more time with his family, resulting in a well-rounded life where he's not only taking care of himself but also nurturing his relationships. His success is proof that his routine works for his career pursuits. But that's not all he has to show for it – he also leads a healthy life that allows him to have exploits beyond running a multi-billion organization.

But is the focus of these routines to communicate that you also need to start your day with an adrenaline rush or a steaming bowl of cereal? Not at all. Instead, it shows you the importance of creating a life that's all-rounded, which allows you to excel beyond your net worth. As such, this chapter will help you understand how ikigai can help you balance it all, from family to health to your personal development goals.

Know What You Want: Goal Setting and Revision.

Routines are not random. Instead, they hinge on what you want out of life in all aspects. For Dwayne "The Rock" Johnson to start his day with an intense workout, he knows that this is important to maintaining his physique and boosting his overall health, which affects his personal and professional exploits. So, the first step to creating a routine is having a goal in mind, which takes us back to the visualization we did in Chapter 3. What does your perfect life look like, and how does this fit into your ikigai?

In this case, we will use Jared, a 40-year-old man who wants to pursue his passion for candle-making as his full-time career. Using the SMART approach discussed in Chapter 2, we can write down his goal: "I want to start a candle-making business and sell my products online through my website. I plan to sell 200 candles within the first four months and will dedicate 30 hours a week to making the candles and managing the website. I plan to launch the website within the next month and will have 50 candles ready for dispatch within this time."

Aside from this career goal, Jared may have personal development goals, such as taking an online course in influencer marketing.

CHAPTER 6: PRACTICAL KAIZEN STRATEGIES FOR EVERY ASPECT OF LIFE

Examples of personal development goals include learning new skills, embracing mindfulness, trying new recipes, etc.

What's your main ikigai goal? Write it down here. You can refer to Chapters 2 and 3 for context on visualization and SMART goal-setting.

_____

_____

_____

_____

What's your main personal development goal? E.g., Jared wants to complete a course in influencer marketing. Yours can be anything that helps you nurture your talents, help you inch closer to your aspirations, or something that adds to the quality of your life.

_____

_____

_____

_____

From the ikigai goal, Jared can then work on his mini-goals. For example, "create and launch a website in four weeks," "make 15 candles in week 1," etc. Breaking down goals into mini-goals follows the same principles we used to create micro habits in Chapter 4. You can use this chapter for more guidance.

_____

_____

_____

_____

From the personal development goal, you will also have mini-goals. In Jared's case, he can take a 4-week influencer marketing course, and he will complete the course per the outline. What are your mini goals?

_____

_____

_____

_____

These mini-goals will go a long way in helping you gauge your progress. For example, each week, Jared can look at the progress of the website and the number of candles he has made to check if he's progressing well. If he's exceeding his goals given the 20-hour work week, he can readjust his goals to bigger ones. If he's struggling, he may need to reconsider some things, e.g., he can ask for help with the website design.

Reflection sessions help you identify areas of improvement and also give you insights on how to set new SMART goals for the next phase of your life.

Set the Pace for Productivity: Structure Your Life

Have you ever noticed that how you start and end your days affects your overall productivity? For example, if you often wake up late and spend time running all over the house to get to work on time, you'll likely feel flustered the whole day as you are rushing to catch up with time. But when you start your day on the right foot, you find that everything seems to fall into place, down to how you retire to rest. So, how can you create a practical routine?

Ask yourself the following questions:

What time will you wake up? – Ideally, it should be the same time each day.

_____

_____

What will you do in the morning to calm your mind? Examples include working out, meditating, stretching, etc.

_____

_____

What will you have for breakfast? At what time will you do this? A healthy start to the day gives your body and mind the fuel they need.

_____

_____

How will you structure your day? E.g., focused work from 10 am to 2 pm, lunch, emails from 3 pm to 5 pm.

_____

_____

When will you interact with your loved ones? Examples include family dinners, video calls, etc.

_____

_____

When will you engage in activities that aid personal growth? Examples are journaling, reading, and learning a new skill.

_____

_____

When will you go to bed? Like waking up, bedtime should ideally be around the same time each day.

_____

_____

CHAPTER 6: PRACTICAL KAIZEN STRATEGIES FOR EVERY ASPECT OF LIFE

Let's set an example schedule for Jared, our aspiring candle maker, as illustrated in this picture. Jared plans to wake up at 8 am., spend the first thirty minutes doing yoga, get ready for the day, and have breakfast at 9 am. with his family. Between 10 am. and 1 pm., he plans on making candles. He will have lunch from 1 pm. to 2 pm., work on his website till 5 pm., and break for the day. At this time (5 pm. to 9 pm.), he will prepare a fresh meal for his family, spend time catching up with his children, and enjoy the meal with his family. He will then journal about his day at 9 pm., spend an hour catching up on his latest course on influencer marketing, and then unwind for the night, ensuring he's asleep by midnight.

What kind of routine incorporates the goals you have set while allowing you to show up for yourself and your loved ones?

Manage Your Time Effectively

A Spinoza (2024) study revealed that while 88% of people have a to-do list, they still struggle with effective time management. Reasons include lack of clear goals, procrastination, distractions, strenuous work schedules, inconsistency in their routines, unwillingness to delegate tasks to other people, and overcommitting to plans. So, while they may know what they want to do, they still fall behind in the long run.

How can you get past this time management block with kaizen? Previous chapters have already covered how you can deal with procrastination, distractions, and unclear goals. Now is the time to refine your schedule using a few kaizen-inspired tips, as follows:

Step 1: Track how you use your time. Many people love saying that "we all have the same 24 hours in a day, yet we get different results." While this notion does not account for limiting factors, we can agree that we all get the same slate. So, where do you spend the most time, and how can you change this to better your results?

Here's how to do your analysis:

What's been taking most of my time?

_____

_____

CHAPTER 6: PRACTICAL KAIZEN STRATEGIES FOR EVERY ASPECT OF LIFE

Which of these activities is not important in my to-do list?

_____

_____

Which of these activities can I eliminate to make better use of my time?

_____

_____

For example, you may find that you often make personal calls at work, which eat into several hours of your time each week. So, by eliminating these calls during work hours, you can actually perform better. Or you may find that you spend at least two hours a day making fresh meals – you can choose to prep your meals over the weekend to cut back on this time.

Step 2: Prioritize your tasks. Use your mini goals to determine what tasks you must accomplish each day, ensuring that they are SMART. For example, you may find that to write your business plan in a week, you must finish one page each day.

Step 3: Create time blocks. Break down your day into time blocks, during which you will work on specific tasks. It's always best to schedule these blocks based on when you are most focused. For example, if you are often most alert in the morning, use this time for the tasks that require your optimal attention, leaving the smaller tasks to the afternoon when you are less attentive. You can leave tasks such as emails, calls, and messages as the last thing you do in the day.

A time-blocked day can look like this:

TIME	ACTIVITY
9 AM. TO 11 AM.	Work on a presentation for client A.
11 AM. TO 1 PM.	Work on a presentation for client B.
1 PM. TO 2 PM.	Lunch break.
2 PM. TO 3 PM.	Respond to emails and calls.
3 PM. TO 4 PM.	Plan tomorrow's schedule.

Step 4: Use time-management software. You might think that you are capable of working for two hours without taking a break. Not only is this physically strenuous, but you may also find that your brain is unable to concentrate for this long at a time. So, how do you remain effective without wasting time? The key lies in using time-management software, which relies on the Pomodoro technique. You start by working for 20 minutes, which is enough time to get into the **flow state** and make progress in your work. Then, you take a break for 5 minutes to stretch your legs, get some water, etc. Then you go in again for another 20 minutes, keeping at this cycle until you go on a 20-minute break. Over time, you can start increasing your focus time by 5 minutes based on how well you have been progressing. One day, you will find that you can go for an hour without needing a break. But no matter

how much you are **in the zone**, always take a break every hour to reduce physical and mental fatigue.

Step 5: Review your progress. Time-management software gives you a breakdown of how you have been spending your time. It's best to check your account at the end of each day and week so you can know where you're doing great and what might need some work.

It all comes back to the balance in Chapter 5 – by managing your time better, you can actually make time for the things that matter most to you.

Learn How to Be in the Present

"Mindfulness gives you time. Time gives you choices. Choices, skillfully made, lead to freedom."

- BHANTE H. GUNARATANA.

Mindfulness and meditation help you be in the present so you can look for answers within rather than focusing on the noise around you. We did a bit of this in Chapter 3 when searching for our passions. But did you know that these techniques are also crucial in regulating your emotions, improving your focus, and calming your mind? There's a reason most therapists recommend these techniques, which you can practice as follows:

Technique 1: Progressive Muscle Relaxation

Feeling tense? This 5-minute exercise helps you release that tension by relaxing the different muscle groups in your body. Proceed as follows:

- **Sit or lie down in a comfortable place** where nobody can disturb you.

- **Close your eyes** and breathe in through your nose, hold your breath for a few seconds, and breathe out through your mouth.

- **Then, breathe in deeply** through your nose as you curl your toes. Hold this position for a few seconds, and then breathe out deeply through your mouth.

- **Use the same sequence** to work through your muscle groups, from your calves to your thighs, buttocks, stomach, back, chest, hands, arms, shoulders, neck, and face. As you do this, take the time to feel as the muscle groups tense and relax till you cover your entire body.

- **Once finished,** assess how you feel. If you think you need more relaxation, start the process again.

Finish your session with deep breaths as you open your eyes and welcome the relaxation that has now taken over your body.

Technique 2: Deep Breathing

Have you ever been in a tough spot and could not figure out how to calm your mind? The answer often lies in deep breathing, a technique that helps you relax so you can be more present and figure out a way forward with more objectivity. Here's how it works.

- **Sit or lie down in a comfortable place. Then close your eyes and relax your body.** If you have time, you can go through progressive muscle relaxation.

- **Breathe in deeply and slowly through your nose** and feel as your stomach rises, counting up to five.

- **Hold your breath while counting up to five.**

- **Breathe out slowly while counting up to five** as you feel . your stomach fall.

- **Repeat this cycle for five minutes,** paying attention to how your stomach rises and falls.

Your mind will likely wander a lot in the first few instances. But you can refocus it by putting a hand over your stomach and paying attention to how it moves up and down with each breath.

Note: In line with kaizen, it's important to practice these techniques regularly to experience their full benefits.

CHAPTER 7:
Overcoming Challenges on the Journey to Ikigai

"Fall seven times, stand up eight."

- Japanese Proverb.

When people talk about Steven Spielberg, they focus on his successes. After all, without him, iconic films like "Jurassic Park" and "Jaws" would not be the gems they are today. He has a way of turning a script into a masterpiece as he looks at things very differently. But while people appreciate this uniqueness today, that was not always the case. In his early days, Spielberg tried to get into the USC School of Cinematic Arts several times with no success – and as you would expect of anyone trying to actualize their dreams, the rejections hurt and even made him question if he would ever cut it as a filmmaker. After all, if he could not convince a film school to embrace his ideas, what of the world? But Spielberg pushed on, one rejection after another, until he finally got his foot in the industry. He refused to let his insecurities get the better of him, and thanks to this resilience, he got to live in his dreams.

Spielberg is not the first person to have ever faced challenges on his way to achieving his passion. Many people have – I have – you probably will face many obstacles, too. The key differentiator when it comes to challenges is what you do when they arise. Do you give in to them, do you fight back, or do you find a way through? In this chapter, I show you how to push through on your path to achieving your ikigai.

Dealing with Obstacles

> *"Too many of us are not living our dreams because we are living our fears."*
>
> - LES BROWN.

Bronnie Ware, a palliative care nurse, spent a lot of time with dying patients and learned a lot from them. In her book, "The Top Five Regrets of the Dying," she wrote that most of her patients wished that they had lived a life that was true to themselves rather than the one that people expected of them. Many life reflection studies have had the same insights, highlighting that many older adults regret not following their passions. Some hold back because they fear failure, others do it to conform to society, others do not want to risk losing their stable incomes, and others cite lack of time as a reason. Unfortunately, this tradeoff results in regret. Is it worth pushing your dreams to

CHAPTER 7: OVERCOMING CHALLENGES ON THE JOURNEY TO IKIGAI

the backseat only for you to pine over what could have been? We can all agree that this is not the best way to spend our last days on this earth.

So, can you think of why you are holding back? This section will help you dig deeper and come out on the other side of this with practical solutions.

Recognizing and Naming Challenges

Whether we want to admit it or not, we all have fears in life. I'd always been sure of myself when I was working in investing. But the first time I wanted to publish a book, I could not bring myself to do it. I kept pushing the publishing date forward because I was afraid that people would not like the book, or they would not think I knew much about logical topics as I had been an investment consultant most of my life, or they would judge me for leaving my career, or hold me to a higher standard because I was now sharing what I had learned. Without knowing it, I let my fears (real and imagined) get in the way, so I kept holding back on completing the book, yet I had done a really great job. I had to challenge myself to face my fears – only then could I get past the blocks and launch what has been one of the most fruitful journeys of my life.

I challenge you to do the same thing. Find what's holding you back and address it. As much as it might be terrifying, it's the best thing you can do for yourself as you pursue your passion. Here's how you do it:

Exercise 1: Identifying the Roadblocks to Your Purpose.

I. **Sit in a quiet space** where you will not get disturbed by other people. Practice some deep breathing, as highlighted in the last Chapter.

II. **Choose one category in your life.** As reiterated often in this book, our lives are multi-dimensional. As such, you will face challenges in different areas of your life. These can be emotional, social, financial, professional, or personal. You'll start by choosing one category in this exercise.

Example. Philip selects his personal life.

III. **List all the challenges you face in the chosen category.** Part of pushing through challenges is being honest with what they are. So, note down your actual challenges, whether this is from what you have observed or what people around you have noted. Also, be specific about the challenges rather than generalizing them.

Example. Philip has a hard time maintaining a healthy diet, has a strained long-distance relationship, and has not had time to get a proper haircut in weeks.

IV. **Prioritize and reflect on the challenges.** How much do the challenges affect your life? Rate them on a scale of 1 to 10, as this helps you know which ones you should address first.

Example. Philip's main challenge is his diet, as it's affecting his health negatively.

V. **Find the root causes.** What factors in your life feed the challenges you are experiencing?

Example. Philip struggles to eat healthy meals as he has a busy work schedule.

VI. **Use kaizen strategies** to come up with a solution that requires you to take small steps toward achieving progress.

Example. Philip can start prepping meals on weekends and carry healthy snacks with him to work.

VII. **Work on one challenge at a time.** While you may want to tackle different problems at once, the easiest and most sustainable way is to climb one mountain at a time. Once you get the hang of things, you can then start stacking your habits to make way for the cue-behavior-reward cycle.

In a template, this exercise will look like this:

CHALLENGE	RANKING	ROOT CAUSE	KAIZEN STRATEGY
A hard time maintaining a healthy diet	9	Busy work schedule	Weekend meal prepping
A strained long-distance relationship	7	Poor communication	Call my partner once each day
No time to get a proper haircut in weeks	4	Poor time management	Put a haircut in my schedule

Can you create the same for yourself?

Managing Self-Doubt.

Imposter syndrome, which comes down to self-doubt, is a very real yet problematic sensation that we all experience at one point or the other. But here's the thing – it does not just happen. It always has a root cause. For example, Michelangelo was his own harshest critic, as he believed that perfection was the only acceptable work of art. So, when he was commissioned to work on the Sistine Chapel ceiling, he refused the job. Here he was, a sculptor who was now expected to work on a paint job. How could he work on something so different and still keep up with his high expectations and those of his patrons? It wasn't until he questioned his reluctance that he realized that the only thing in his way was himself. And if you've ever set your eyes on the frescoes of the Sistine Chapel, you can agree that this was one of the most beautiful things he ever worked on.

So, are you, like Michelangelo, getting in your own way? The only way to find out is to question where this doubt stems from. Here is how you do it:

Exercise 2: Exploring Your Beliefs

Beliefs set the pace for how we live our lives. In fact, Henry Ford once said, "Whether you believe you can or you can't, you are right." For example, a friend at my previous job was always reluctant to apply for promotions while the rest of us were busy targeting any upward growth we could get. It turns out that, growing up, his father would often tell him that "they were average people, and that's all they would ever be."

Subconsciously, he had embraced these limiting beliefs, not knowing how impactful they were in his decisions.

Can you pinpoint the source of your doubts? Answering the following questions can help you unearth where the self-doubt began.

What past experiences have made you feel like you are incapable of doing a great job? Why? (Remember all the times you have felt like you were not good enough. What was happening? Why did you feel that way?)

_____

_____

_____

_____

What situations make you doubt yourself? Why? (Think of social and professional settings where you have felt like you do not belong.)

_____

_____

_____

_____

Which people contribute to this self-doubt? How? (It could be people you interact with, the kind of media you consume, etc.)

_____

_____

Journaling the answers to these questions will shed more light on why you are feeling the way you do. Try to be as honest with yourself as possible.

Exercise 3: Challenging Your Thinking.

It's one thing to know where your beliefs stem from. It's another to challenge them to change your way of thinking. How can you do this? – Through **The source-validity approach**. My therapist (yes, I have been to therapy) once walked me through a simple way to work through any negative perceptions I come across:

Step 1: Is it true based on what you know (facts, not opinions)?

Step 2: Is the source trustworthy?

Step 3: Can you back the thought with evidence?

Step 4: Does it make logical sense?

Step 5: What is the intention behind it?

So, let's see this in action. Take Sam, for example. He wants to start a flower shop but holds back because someone tells him there is no market for such a business. Sam knows that the market trends have pointed to a gap in the market, and his business can actually succeed. With just step 1, he can discount the self-doubt raised by this other person. But what if he did not have the market data? He would move on to the second step – is this information coming from someone he can trust? If not, he would take the information with a grain of salt and move on to the third step, where he would look at market data.

The idea here is not to ignore information that you come across. Instead, it is to challenge the thoughts that cross your mind or those others share based on their evidence. As a lawyer would say, if the shoe does not fit, then you must acquit.

Exercise 4: Using positive affirmations.

Every day, I start my morning with affirmations – I have a list that I go through that speaks to my limiting beliefs. For example, I always believed that I had to earn everything, from a 5-minute break from work to a fun weekend with friends – everything required justification. So, one of my affirmations reads, "Me to me – anything for you," reminding me that I deserve the good things. I don't need to earn them.

How can you use this approach to change your thinking?

Step 1: List your limiting beliefs. This list will grow over time, but you can now work with what you have now. For example, your limiting belief may be "I am not likable enough to run a successful café."

Step 2: Change your limiting beliefs into affirmations. In our example above, you can change this to "I have an inviting personality. People like me for who I am."

Step 3: Make affirmation cards for each of the beliefs you have written down. It can even be on simple pieces of paper that you put in a jar.

Step 4: Affirm yourself every day. Randomly choose one of the affirmations and say them out loudly to yourself in the mirror. It might sound cheesy, but it works. Soon enough, you'll be so comfortable with this process that you will have no qualms about repeating the words in front of people.

Over time, you will find that your beliefs no longer hold you back as you start to believe in the possibilities. That is the power of positive thinking!

Exercise 5: Embracing Gratitude.

Self-doubt often creeps in because of the expectations we put on ourselves. For example, if you think that the only way to be successful is if you have a garage full of the latest cars, a mansion, a top-paying position, and a membership to the top clubs in the country, you will feel inadequate until you have these things. But what if you were to embrace what you have now and take pride in it? You'd have a much better outlook on life.

Gratitude helps you recognize all the ways you stand out and how blessed you are, no matter how little you think you have. Eventually, you learn how to be content as you work for what else you could have. So, how does it work?

- **Make a list of all your strengths.** E.g., I am an amazing cook. Use exercise 4 in section 1 of Chapter 3 to help you with this.

- **Write down all the things you love about yourself** – these are qualities rather than strengths, e.g., I love that I listen to other people and care about what they have to say.

- **Note all your accomplishments, whether personal or professional**, e.g., I ran my first ever 5k and got a participation medal.

Update your list often. In fact, for gratitude, this is best done as a daily practice such that you highlight all your successes at the end of each day. It makes you feel fulfilled about what you are doing and gives you the push to try harder the next day.

Finding Motivation When It Wanes

"The greatest glory in living lies not in never falling, but in rising every time we fall."

- Nelson Mandela.

Vincent van Gogh is one of the most revered artists today. But did you know that he only sold one painting in his lifetime? Yet even with this setback, he kept on working on his art as he believed in it, and it was a source of joy for him. Sir James Dyson is another great example of someone who kept at it despite challenges. It took 5,126 failed prototypes and 15 years of hard work for him to create something that took the world by storm. So, am I advocating for you to sacrifice your life in pursuit of your passion? No. Instead, these and other amazing people serve as an example of how much perseverance can pay off in the end. But how do you stick to your path?

Revisit Your Why

Progression may be fulfilling, but it is also challenging. So, you will likely wake up one day and start questioning your choices. Why are you waking up at 6 am every day? Why are you spending two hours each day working on that website? Why, why, why? If you cannot answer this question, you will likely give in to the temptation that lies in wait, be it procrastination, engaging in a distraction, etc. So, how can you get ahead of this?

1. **Create a vision board,** as shown in Chapter 3. It will serve as a visual reminder of why you are working per your schedule.

2. **Have regular checkpoints.** Ideally, you will reflect on your goals and current progress every week and month to keep up with your mini-goals.

3. **Set reminders** to get you back to speed every day. For example, your alarm sound can be a voice note of you reminding yourself what you are working for and why. You can also use sticky notes, phone wallpapers, and other sensory reminders.

Do not let yourself lose sight of the final goal.

Improve Yourself – The Benefits of Reassessment and Adaptation

When J.K. Rowling wrote the first Harry Potter book and had it published, she was thrilled. She'd had 12 publishers reject her ideas, and Bloomsbury had finally given her a chance to prove herself. So, rather than soak in this success and follow the same path, she opted to ensure that the plot and characters evolved to keep the audience guessing, resulting in one of the best series of all time. Without this dedication, her star would likely have faded after the first few books.

You are amazing, just the way you are. But that's not to say that you do not have room to improve yourself. Embrace a growth mindset where you open yourself up to learning new things as you step outside of what you know. Gradually, as explained in Chapter 4, try new things and see where they take you. It may not look like much at the time, but it soon adds up, resulting in you being successful in achieving your goals.

Build a Community Around You

Remember the "moai" concept in ikigai? You will need a community as you work towards your purpose. But the goal is not just to have people around you. Instead, it is to create a community of people who add positivity to your life. How?

- **Nurture positive relationships.** You are the average of the people you spend most of your time with - Look at the people around you. Are they bringing you down and adding to your self-doubt? Are they your source of comfort and joy? Cling to the people who make you feel heard and seen, and avoid those who introduce doubt or negativity in your life.

- **Find mentors who can support you**. You will face many challenges as you work towards your new career path. You don't have to do it alone. Mentorship can come from people you interact with, or you can seek guidance from online coaches or other people who have the resources to help you improve. For example, if you want to be a financial coach, you can follow one online and get insights into how they run their business, what value they offer, etc., even if you don't get to meet them in person.

- **Use online communities to your benefit**. We live in a time when you can find your community online, be it discussion forums or social media. Look for spaces where you can find people who share your passions so that you can learn from them and get inspiration. You can also use these spaces to share your goals so that you can get encouragement from people who understand just how important your goals are to you.

- **Be open about how you feel**. Self-doubt often gets the better of people because they let it eat away at them while they remain silent. Don't let this be the case. Sometimes, even with journaling, you may find that your fears may derail you from self-improvement. It's advisable to reach out for help, be it from family or friends you can trust. I also encourage you to try therapy, especially if your attitudes are rooted deeply in your experiences.

Finally, be compassionate to yourself. Most times, we say things to ourselves that we would not say to other people. We may be echoing what others have said to us or expressing our disappointment of not measuring up to the standards we have for ourselves. This harshness does not help as it only erodes your confidence even more, robbing you of the chance to derive happiness from what you have now. You will get better results by treating yourself with kindness, forgiving yourself for the mistakes you have made, and taking the time to take care of your health.

Embracing Uncertainty

"Go for it now. The future is promised to no one."
- WAYNE DYER.

Vera Wang was 40 years old when she quit her career as a journalist and figure skater to start designing bridal wear. Raymond Chandler was 44 when he wrote his first detective novel, having lost his job in the Great Depression. I was 40 when I left my career and chose to throw myself into the world of philosophy. Is the theme here that life begins at 40? Not quite. The headline here is that many people reach a point where they leave what they know behind and enter a new realm, whether it's a complete turnaround or a pivot. And while this can be exciting, it is also a terrifying time that comes with a lot of uncertainty. Here is how you can navigate this new scene:

Learn to Let Go of Expectations

People often start their journeys with a clear goal, hoping everything falls into place. Unfortunately, these assumptions can result in disappointment. Say, for example, that you are opening a new restaurant and are expecting a turnout of 200 guests. If 150 people show up, how will you feel? How about if 100 people show up?

You cannot always control what happens. Uncertainty is a part of life, and as you embark on any journey, you have to embrace the fact that you will experience challenges that you may not have even thought about. For instance, who could ever have predicted that the world would experience a pandemic that forced people to stay home for months on end? That's life – it's uncertain. But there are two things that you can manage – your intentions and flexibility.

Intentions refer to what you hope to achieve without setting out a specific outcome. For example, your intention can be to open a restaurant with a 200-person seating. In this case, you will focus on the process of opening the restaurant and the actions you can control, such as the menu, the theme, the staffing, etc. By releasing the need for things to turn out a certain way, you can let go of the pressure and actually enjoy the process. So, whether 50 or 250 people show up, you will have followed your intentions.

CHAPTER 7: OVERCOMING CHALLENGES ON THE JOURNEY TO IKIGAI

Flexibility looks at how willing you are to accept different outcomes and your reactions to changes. Say, for example, that your intention is to open your restaurant in a week's time, but the permit process is taking too long. When you are flexible, you are able to adjust your opening to account for such a change without thinking of the launch as having been ruined.

So, in all things, ask yourself – are you setting intentions or expectations? Are you open to different outcomes?

Embrace a Growth Mindset: Choose Progress over Perfection.

In the previous chapters, I talked about the need to set smaller goals that fit into your ikigai as a whole. For example, your goal can be to run a meal-delivery service that caters to office workers who want healthy meals at affordable prices. And you can make it SMART (Specific, Measurable, Achievable, Relevant, and Time-bound) such that you want to set up an app in the next 6 months, target 100 customers in the first month, etc.

The best way to enjoy your journey is to break your goals into smaller milestones. Each time you achieve growth, celebrate it, as this shows progress. And whenever you make mistakes, aim to learn from them instead of beating yourself about them. Mistakes are actually opportunities for growth. For example, if you set up an app that people do not like because it is too heavy, you will learn that people want a simple app. Then, you can build on this to create a better version.

Most importantly, just start working on your goals. As Carrie Fisher once said, *"Stay afraid but do it anyway. What's important is the action. You don't have to wait to be confident. Just do it, and eventually, the confidence will follow."*

CHAPTER 8:
The 21-Day Plan to Master Your Ikigai with Kaizen

"Change is hard at first, messy in the middle, and gorgeous at the end."

- ROBIN SHARMA.

We've covered a lot of ground in the last seven chapters, and you may be wondering how it all comes together. Well, like with kaizen, we will take it all one day at a time, focusing our efforts on making small, gradual changes so that in just 21 days, you will have the complete blueprint to achieve your ikigai. Follow this section as it has been laid out so you can build a strong foundation that you can always come back to long after you have started your journey.

Note: To make this section easier to follow, I will use the example of Duncan, a 37-year-old hotel manager.

Week 1 – Laying the Foundation for Your 21-Day Journey

"You are what you do, not what you say you do."

- Carl Jung.

Many people get stuck on talking about their hopes and dreams but do not actually put in the work to actualize them. This week, we will get your plan in motion by taking on manageable yet impactful tasks as follows:

Day 1: Planning Your First Week

The saying goes that "by failing to plan, you plan to fail." Day 1 is all about setting the tone for the rest of your week by focusing on the following aspects:

1. **Essential Preparation Steps.**

    You will not need much to get started on your ikigai. But to ensure you have the right materials to work on everything we will cover this week, set out the following:

    - *A journal. It can be a plain book.*

    - *A pen or pencil. You can add colored pencils if you like artsy presentations.*

    - *A laptop or desktop computer.*

    - *A timer. You can also use your phone or clock for this.*

In addition to these items, you will need to set out a space in your home or office where you will work on the exercises in this chapter. A desk and chair will be enough. Ensure it's a comfortable space where you can enjoy privacy and will not experience any distractions for about thirty minutes at a time.

Example. Duncan has an office at home. As such, all he needs is a book, a pen, his personal laptop, and his phone, and he is good to go.

2. **Time Management**

   You must invest time in each of the week's activities if you are to progress sustainably throughout the three weeks. But how much time will you need? Ideally, you should carve out at least two hours of your day to work on the day's activity. You can do the task in one two-hour block or can split your hours into 30-minute or one-hour blocks during the day, based on what works for you.

   There is no set period, so you can do this in the morning, afternoon, or even evening. However, structure is important in this journey. Refer to Section 1 of Chapter 6, under "**Set the pace for productivity**" and "**Manage your time effectively.**" These sections will help you create time blocks to work on the week's activities while ensuring you still have time for work and other responsibilities.

   Example. Duncan works from 8 am to 8 pm. As such, he will need to carve out time outside these hours to work on his ikigai. Given that he gets home at 8:30 pm having had dinner at the hotel, he can choose to work on his daily tasks from 9:00 pm to 11:00 pm. So, his schedule will look like this.

TIME	7 AM TO 7:30 AM	7:30 AM TO 8 AM	8 AM TO 1 PM	1 PM TO 2 PM	2 PM TO 8 PM
TASK	Get ready for work	Commute to work	At work	Have lunch	At work
TIME	8 PM TO 8:30 PM	8:30 PM TO 9 PM	9 PM TO 11 PM	11 PM TO 12 AM	
TASK	Commute home	Shower	Ikigai and kaizen tasks	Wind down for bed	

Use the same strategy to figure out what works best for you by factoring in all your other responsibilities. For example, you may find that it's better for you to carve out one hour in the morning and one in the evening.

3. **Daily Rituals**

This week, we will focus on two daily rituals that you will integrate into your schedule moving forward. Which are they?

a. **Daily reflective journaling**. Head to Exercise 1 in Section 1 of Chapter 3, which relates to reflective journaling. Ensure you do some journaling in the morning, noon, and evening, averaging at least five minutes each time.

CHAPTER 8: THE 21-DAY PLAN TO MASTER YOUR IKIGAI WITH KAIZEN

Example. Duncan can journal for five minutes when he wakes up at 7:00 am., again at 1:00 pm. at work, and at 11:00 pm. when he finishes his daily ikigai and kaizen tasks.

b. **Gratitude highlights.** Refer to Exercise 5 in Section 1 of Chapter 7. Then, every morning, take five minutes to write down three things you are grateful for, be it health, family, friends, a career, etc.

Example. Duncan can write down his gratitude highlights after his morning journaling.

You can set a reminder on your phone or leave your journal out as a cue to engage in these exercises. It's also important to include these exercises in your schedule. Let's use Duncan's example to illustrate how to go about this.

TIME	7 AM TO 7:30 AM	7:30 AM TO 8 AM	8 AM TO 1 PM	1 PM TO 2 PM	2 PM TO 8 PM
TASK	Get ready for work	Commute to work	At work	Have lunch	At work
	Morning reflections			Noon reflections	
	Gratitude highlights				

TIME	8 PM TO 8:30 PM	8:30 PM TO 9 PM	9 PM TO 11 PM	11 PM TO 12 AM	
TASK	Commute home	Shower	Ikigai and kaizen tasks	Wind down for bed	
			Evening reflections		

See how it integrates even the small tasks? Do the same in your schedule.

Day 2: Mapping Out Your Passions and Interests.

Our work today will focus on finding your passions and interests. As such, head to Section 1 in Chapter 3 and work on the following exercises:

  a. Exercise 2 on self-reflection.

  b. Exercise 3 on interest inventory.

  c. Exercise 4 on strengths and skills.

  d. Exercise 5 on visualization.

These exercises will likely take anything from 20 to 30 minutes each. You will also need to continue with the daily self-reflections and gratitude highlights.

Day 3: Mapping Your Four-Circle Diagram

Today, we draw closer to your ikigai. Head to section 2 of Chapter 3 and follow the prompts to find the intersections between your passion, mission, vocation, and profession. Complete the framework and write down the paths that are viable per your assessment. This activity can take anything from one to three hours. Do not rush it, as the result influences everything else for the next few weeks.

Example. Upon reflection, Duncan realizes that he has a passion for organizing excursions. Moreover, there is a growing market for this service, and he already has a network he can rely on to build his business. His passion passes all the intersections and is thus viable.

Day 4: Setting Your Goals

What are you aiming to achieve? What small steps must you take to get there? You will find the answers to these questions in Section 2 of Chapter 3, titled "Your Reality Versus Your Ikigai." Use your overall vision to create SMART goals, and then break them down into smaller and more manageable tasks. Then, choose how you will reward yourself for meeting your goals.

Example. Duncan wishes to start a tour business. But to do this, he has to register the business, open a website, quit his current job, market his services to tourists, etc. It's a long journey, and he has a 6-month plan between now and his official launch. In the first week, he wishes to open a website, the reward for which will be a new shirt he's wanted to buy for a long time.

Day 5: Introducing Kaizen to Your Life

Now, we are on to Chapter 4. What habits in your life are holding you back? Complete the following exercises in Chapter 4:

    a. Exercise 1 in Section 1: Recognizing Your Triggers.

    b. Exercise 2 in Section 1: Substituting Your Bad Behaviors.

    c. Exercise 1 in Section 2: Creating Your Micro Habits

    d. Exercise 2 in Section 2: The Reminder-Routine-Reward Cycle.

    e. Exercise 3 in Section 2: Tracking Your Micro Habits.

These exercises will average 30 minutes each. Choose something small that you will work on every day, e.g., I will drink one glass of water each day. Then, add this to the same schedule with mini goals and tasks, and choose a reward for accomplishing your habit.

Example. Duncan wishes to offer the tours himself. But to do this, he has to be fit. His assessment highlights that he leads a highly sedentary life. He chooses to start taking a 20-minute walk during his lunch break to prepare himself. As a reward for sticking to this habit, he will catch the week's movie in the cinema.

Other examples of habits you can try to adopt are "doing 10 jumping jacks each day," "spending 5 minutes tidying up your room each day," and "spending 10 minutes reading a book each day." The key is to find something that relates to your ikigai. Keep it small for now – we are just getting started.

CHAPTER 8: THE 21-DAY PLAN TO MASTER YOUR IKIGAI WITH KAIZEN

Day 6: Practicing Mindfulness

Your beliefs play a huge role in shaping your journey. As such, it's best to tackle them from the start using the exercises below from Chapter 7:

   a. Exercise 1 in Section 1: Identifying the roadblocks to your purpose.

   b. Exercise 2 in Section 1: Exploring your beliefs.

   c. Exercise 4 in Section 1: Using positive affirmations.

These exercises will average 20 to 30 minutes each. Take your time with them.

Example. Duncan has always held back from starting his business because he's afraid of losing his stable and guaranteed monthly income. After all, when running a business, he'll not have a specific sum of money coming in every month, will be responsible for making ends meet, and will have additional business overheads. Much of this fear comes from having seen his parents lose their savings in an economic downturn. However, he's willing to push past the fear with affirmations such as "I am creating the life of my dreams."

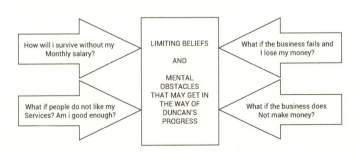

A snapshot of what goes on in Duncan's mind.

Day 7: Being Present

It's been a long week. How about you connect with yourself a bit more? Head to the following exercises in Section 2 in Chapter 6:

a. Progressive muscle relaxation.

b. Deep breathing.

These should take about 10 to 20 minutes. Once you are feeling settled, head back to Exercise 1 and Exercise 2 in Section 1 of Chapter 3. Now is the time to enjoy some reflective journaling and meditation to assess your highs and lows while checking if you still feel aligned with your ikigai. These exercises will be integral in your journey long after the 21-day plan, so be sure to make time for them.

Additional exercise for the day: It's time for your weekly review. Use exercise 1 of section 1 in Chapter 3 to highlight your week's activities and how you have felt about them. Are you feeling like you are closer to your goals now?

Week 2 – Building Consistency: Essential Daily Routines for a Life of Purpose

"Every day, do something that will inch you closer to a better tomorrow."

- DOUG FIREBAUGH.

CHAPTER 8: THE 21-DAY PLAN TO MASTER YOUR IKIGAI WITH KAIZEN

By now, you have a clear idea of what you are working toward and the obstacles that may get in your way. Let's streamline your activities to create a sustainable routine that you can follow.

Days 8 to 13

These days will build on the foundation from the first week and will hinge on creating lasting habits that you can lean on going forward. As such, they will feature the same structure to get you into that reminder-routine-reward cycle. Using Duncan as our example once again, let's see how this will play out:

Morning Routine (10 to 30 minutes).

You do not need to start waking up at 5 am. or having cereal as the first thing when you wake up. It's all about making small changes with positive results. So, all you need is to create time for the following activities each day:

a. **Gratitude highlights (5 minutes)**. Review your life and write down three things you are grateful to have. These highlights are personal to you. While one person may be grateful for having a car because it allows them to commute easily, another may be grateful for sunny weather because they've been battling seasonal depression. So, what are you grateful for today?

b. **Deep breathing or meditation (5 to 10 minutes)**. Mindfulness helps steer you toward enjoying the present rather than dwelling on the past or agonizing over the future. Take some time to enjoy some deep breaths or connect with why you are pursuing your goals.

c. **Reviewing the day's goals (5 to 10 minutes)**. You always want to know what you are working toward. In this case, you will have two goals which you set on Day 4 and Day 5 of week 1, as follows:

- **Your ikigai mini goals**. These are the small tasks that you must accomplish each day to meet your weekly, monthly, and overall targets.

    Example. This week, Duncan is working on setting up his website. So, each day, he has a specific task to complete, as follows:

DAY	1	2	3	4
TASK	Choose domain name	Pay for website hosting	Design website logo	Create website menu
	Choose website host	Create website account	Create website tags	Customize homepage
	Choose website niche	Choose website theme	Create website slogan	Write homepage content

CHAPTER 8: THE 21-DAY PLAN TO MASTER YOUR IKIGAI WITH KAIZEN

DAY	5	6	7	
TASK	Create services	Create blog page	Add services content	
	Add services to menu	Customize blog page		
	Write services content			

- **Your micro habits.** What are you working on this week? Keep in mind that it's best to start with one habit before stacking it, as explained in Chapter 4. In Duncan's case, he will be working on being more active by taking a 20-minute walk for three days a week during lunch. What's yours?

d. **Morning reflections (5 to 10 minutes).** These tie back to Exercise 1 in Section 1 of Chapter 3, where you ask yourself what you are most excited about doing for the day. While you have found your passion and its intersections, it's important to gauge how you feel about your day's activities to check if they align with what fulfills you.

Your morning routine is an easy way to remind yourself what you need to do and why it's important. Set aside about 10 to 30 minutes for this.

Midday Routine (5 to 10 minutes).

Once the day starts, it can be hard to find the time to connect with your ikigai. But it's important to remain grounded, which you can do by finding five to ten minutes to reflect on your day. Ask yourself the following questions:

- What has been the highlight of my day so far?
- What have I learned about myself?
- What am I most excited about doing the rest of the day?
- Are there any areas that may need extra work?
- Are you feeling aligned with your purpose?

It helps to practice some deep breathing before answering these questions in your journal, as it helps clear your mind. If you are unsure how to get these five to ten minutes, you can schedule this check-in during lunch.

Example. Duncan gets a one-hour lunch break from 1 pm. to 2 pm. During this time, he plans to get his lunch, eat it outside where he can enjoy the sun, and take a walk around the hotel for 20 minutes. Then, at 1:40 pm., he will return to his office, lock the door to avoid disturbances, and take 5 to 10 minutes to review his day. Even with a busy schedule, he can still keep tabs on how he's progressing per his goals.

CHAPTER 8: THE 21-DAY PLAN TO MASTER YOUR IKIGAI WITH KAIZEN

Evening Routine.

At the end of the day, it's important to check in with yourself to see how well you did. It's all about being honest with yourself so you can give yourself a better chance of succeeding as the weeks continue, as follows:

a. **Reflective journaling (5 to 10 minutes).** Take the time to look back on your day. What activities did you enjoy the most? How would you rate your day? What were your highs and lows? Did you put in the work necessary to achieve your ikigai?

Example. Duncan bought a new pair of walking shoes to help him enjoy his walks more. On the low side, he was stuck in traffic for over half an hour, which ate into his ikigai and kaizen time.

b. **Progress tracking (5 to 10 minutes).** Each day, look at the mini goals and micro habits that you were to work on – did you hit your target?

Example. Duncan's mini goal for day 1 was to choose a domain name, website host, and website niche. He's managed to do all three, resulting in a 100% score. For his micro habit, he was to walk 20 minutes at noon, and he did that, which is another 100%.

As such, his progress tracking can look like this for his mini goals. You can create a similar table in your journal or use the worksheets in the appendix.

DAY	1	2	3	4
TASK	Choose domain name	Pay for website hosting	Design website logo	Create website menu
	Choose website host	Create website account	Create website tags	Customize homepage
	Choose website niche	Choose website theme	Create website slogan	Write homepage content
DONE?	3 out of 3 (100%)			
DAY	5	6	7	
TASK	Create services	Create blog page	Add services content	
	Add services to menu	Customize blog page		
	Write services content			

And on his micro habits, it can look like this:

DAY	1	2	3	4
TASK	Walk for 20 minutes	Rest	Walk for 20 minutes	Rest
DONE?	√			

CHAPTER 8: THE 21-DAY PLAN TO MASTER YOUR IKIGAI WITH KAIZEN

DAY	5	6	7	
TASK	Rest	Rest	Walk for 20 minutes	
DONE?				

Every day that he goes on his walk, he will add a tick under the "Done" row, and every time he fails to go on the walk, he will mark it with an "x," as I will later show you.

Tracking your progress each day will help you see how well you are doing, which motivates you to keep going or work harder, which aligns with the kaizen principles in Chapter 2.

c. **Setting the next day's goals (5 to 10 minutes).** What mini goals and micro habits await you? The habits will largely remain the same unless you choose to stack them after you have successfully integrated one habit into your life. But the goals will often change. For example, Duncan will work on a different aspect of his website each day. What about you?

d. **Identifying areas that need work (5 to 10 minutes).** Practice Kaizen by identifying one minor task to improve today. But how do you find it? It's all about looking at how well you are progressing. Is your schedule working? Are you learning things about yourself that require your attention? Reflect on these aspects and choose the thing that stands out the most to you, focusing on one thing at a time.

Example. Duncan has realized that he has a lot of negative self-talk. So, he's going to add positive affirmations to his schedule to remind himself of his worth. Once again, his schedule will change to this one, which has positive affirmations during his commutes.

TIME	7 AM TO 7:30 AM	7:30 AM TO 8 AM	8 AM TO 1 PM	1 PM TO 2 PM
TASK	Get ready for work	Commute to work	At work	Have lunch
	Morning reflections	Positive affirmations		Noon reflections
	Gratitude highlights			Take 20 minute walk
	Deep Breathing/ Meditation			
	Daily goal reviews			
TIME	8 PM TO 8:30 PM	8:30 PM TO 9 PM	9 PM TO 11 PM	11 PM TO 12 AM
TASK	Commute home	Shower	Ikigai and kaizen task	Wind down for bed
	Positive affirmations		Evening reflections	

Your schedule does not have to be packed with activities. In fact, for the first few weeks, it's best to focus on one micro habit, your ikigai goals, and your morning, noon, and evening routines.

Points to Note.

It's a learning curve. The first few weeks will likely be challenging as you try to integrate new habits into your life. Sometimes, you may not be in the mood to stick to the schedule, and at others, you may even question why you're keeping up with these habits. But in the face of these challenges, it's important to keep going. Only then can these activities start feeling more natural, drawing you closer to the life you envision.

There are no hard and fast rules. Not all the exercises in this plan are mandatory. You may find that some do not work for you or are too challenging. It's okay to tweak the exercises to find the pace that works for you so that you can enjoy the process. For example, you may find that you prefer doing your gratitude highlights in the evening as this is when you can really lean into the process - that's okay. The goal here is to choose a habit (even if it means replacing something in the plan) and stick to it, cultivating a routine that you can follow in the long term.

Remember: Easy does it.

Day 14

On this last day of the second week, you will continue with your morning, noon, and evening routines as well as your micro habits. But you will also review your entire week. So, what does this look like?

a. **What accomplishments did you have?** These can be anything from your micro habits to your mini goals. For example, Duncan's accomplishment can be, "I set up my travel website."

What are yours?

_____

_____

_____

_____

b. **What challenges did you face?** Write down all the obstacles you faced, be they physical, emotional, etc. For example, Duncan has a fear of losing his guaranteed income once he starts a business, what with the extra business expenses and the risks that come with running a business. And he may have allowed this fear to get in the way of working on his website.

_____

_____

_____

_____

CHAPTER 8: THE 21-DAY PLAN TO MASTER YOUR IKIGAI WITH KAIZEN

c. **What lessons have you learned from your accomplishments?** How about your wins?

_____

_____

_____

_____

d. **Did you meet your ikigai goals?** How many out of the 7 days were you on track?

_____

_____

_____

_____

Example: Duncan accomplished everything in his schedule and is now able to move on to the next phase of his website creation. Moreover, he can now get the shirt he wanted as his **reward**.

e. **Did you meet your micro habit goals?** How many of the 7 days were you on track?

_____

_____

_____

_____

For example, Duncan's progress may be 2 out of 3 days of the week, as shown below. In this case, he will not get the **reward** he wanted and can move it to be a reward for the next week.

DAY	1	2	3	4
TASK	Walk for 20 minutes	Rest	Walk for 20 minutes	Rest
DONE?	√		√	
DAY	5	6	7	
TASK	Rest	Rest	Walk for 20 minutes	
DONE?			X	

f. **Are your priorities aligned with your ikigai?** It's important to assess how you are spending your time and whether this is helping you achieve your goals. For example, Duncan may realize that staying out late on Sundays makes it hard for him to start his Monday on the right foot. So, he may opt to call it a night earlier than usual the next time he goes out. What about you?

_____

_____

_____

_____

CHAPTER 8: THE 21-DAY PLAN TO MASTER YOUR IKIGAI WITH KAIZEN

g. **What goals should you target in the coming week?** The key is to keep your goals SMART, even as you note progress. If you are moving faster than you thought, you can pick up the pace to challenge yourself. If you are moving as expected and do not feel like you are sitting on your skills, you can continue on the path you had chosen. But if you are falling behind, focus on addressing the challenges you are facing before stacking your habits or goals. You always want to have a solid foundation to ensure your growth is sustainable. So, what are your targets for the next week?

_____

_____

_____

_____

Example: Duncan's goals can look like this for his ikigai. His reward, this time, can be his favorite croissant from the local café.

DAY	1	2	3	4
TASK	Write blog 1	Create pictures for blog 1	Post blog 1	Create pictures for blog 2
			Write blog 2	
DONE?				

DAY	5	6	7	
TASK	Post blog 2	Create pictures for blog 3	Post blog 3	
	Write blog 3		Write blog 4	
DONE?				

Example. His micro habits can look like the picture below as he did not accomplish his goal last time. The focus this week will be on setting this foundation. Since he did not get his reward the last time, he can choose to still aim for another movie at the cinema.

DAY	1	2	3	4
TASK	Walk for 20 minutes	Rest	Walk for 20 minutes	Rest
DONE?				
DAY	5	6	7	
TASK	Rest	Rest	Walk for 20 minutes	
DONE?				

Weekly check-ins are an essential part of your journey. Keep at them every week, as it's the best way to measure how well you are doing in the long run.

CHAPTER 8: THE 21-DAY PLAN TO MASTER YOUR IKIGAI WITH KAIZEN

Week 3 – Expanding and Reinforcing: Sustaining Habits Long-Term

*"There are only two rules for being successful.
One, figure out exactly what you want to do, and two, do it."*

- Mario Cuomo.

Great job on making it to the third week. So, what can you expect this week?

1. **Stick to the morning, noon, and evening routines.** The only way to keep reflections, gratitude highlights, and meditation as habits is to keep doing them until they feel like second nature. So, your schedule this week will almost mirror what you had the previous week.

   Take a look at Duncan's week plan below. As you can see, we are sticking to the affirmations that he started in the previous week so that they can align with his commute. He's also still working on his website every day after work.

TIME	7 AM TO 7:30 AM	7:30 AM TO 8 AM	8 AM TO 1 PM	1 PM TO 2 PM
TASK	Get ready for work	Commute to work	At work	Have lunch
	Morning reflections	Positive affirmations		Noon reflections
	Gratitude highlights			Take 20 minute walk
	Deep Breathing/ Meditation			
	Daily goal reviews			

TIME	8 PM TO 8:30 PM	8:30 PM TO 9 PM	9 PM TO 11 PM	11 PM TO 12 AM
TASK	Commute home	Shower	Website work	Wind down for bed
	Positive affirmations		Evening reflections	

2. **Challenge yourself to be better.** What kaizen actions have you chosen for yourself? Say, for example, that you chose to work on becoming a better timekeeper. Challenge yourself to stick to this for personal and professional events. Use any chance you can get to improve yourself.

For example, Duncan's goal is to get fitter by taking a 20-minute walk at lunchtime. But that doesn't mean he can't work his walking habit into other areas, like taking the stairs instead of the lift and parking his car far from the hotel entrance so he can get more steps.

Note: Be careful not to overdo the challenge, as this can have the opposite of the desired effect. Always seek a balance between being too intense and being complacent.

3. **Get an accountability partner.** There are different ways to measure your progress with someone else watching you, as follows:

    - **Get a mentor.** Find someone who you can trust to help elevate you, be it personally or professionally. For example, Duncan can seek advice from a tour expert on his business. This expert can also review his progress and let him know if he's on the right track.

    - **Share your journey with a friend or family member.** Make sure it's someone who can point out where you are going wrong. It's all about honesty.

    - **Use an app.** There are many apps that can help you gauge your progress. For example, a habit tracker app can help Duncan log his walking time. The app will show him his progress and notify him when he is falling behind.

    Even with an accountability partner, keep up with your daily and weekly check-ins.

4. **Maintain your work-life balance.** It's now time to go back to Chapter 5 and assess how well you are integrating your ikigai with the rest of your life. Are you making time for

yourself? How about your loved ones? Don't get so caught up in achieving perfection that you ignore the importance of prioritization and me-time.

5. **Remain flexible**. Remember what we said in Chapter 7? Even with the best plans, you cannot control everything that happens in life. Keep setting your intentions while leaving room to adapt to changing situations.

Keep up with the weekly and quarterly reviews. As you do so, don't forget to **reward yourself, challenge yourself, tie your efforts to your ikigai**, and **give yourself grace** as you keep on working on yourself. It's a journey, and you've only just begun –keep going.

Note.

Refer to one previous chapter every week to help you remain grounded as to why you are working on yourself. These chapters will also serve as resources for what to do when you are feeling stuck in any area of your life, be it time management to boundaries to communication.

Take that First Step Today

"Take the first step in faith. You don't have to see the whole staircase; just take the first step."

- Martin Luther King Jr.

Remember the story of my friend at the start of this book? After I shared my journey with her, she took a while to rethink her

CHAPTER 8: THE 21-DAY PLAN TO MASTER YOUR IKIGAI WITH KAIZEN

life. She was unsure about leaving her high-flying career. After all, it came with all the perks she had ever wanted – the private schools, nice neighborhoods, country club memberships, first-class tickets around the world, you name it. But even with all these things, she knew she wasn't happy – she was succeeding at chasing a dream that was not hers.

Eventually, she gave in to the idea of something different. And boy, did she go all in! After years of uncovering her passion and fighting the urge to maintain the status quo, she finally went back to the one thing she had loved as a child – crocheting. She set up a yarn shop where she sells all kinds of knitting materials and also teaches other people how to crochet and knit. And I can truly say that she's a different person from the lady who could barely enjoy the beauty of Dubai. Now, her eyes light up when she talks about what she does. She's always making something for someone she loves and is always eager to teach people how to handcraft. Her business is doing well, she gets to spend more time with her family, she has created a community that she loves, and most importantly, she's happy – and that's all that matters.

So, am I saying that you've got to start from scratch if you want to pursue your ikigai? Not at all. You can choose to start small as you integrate your passion with your existing life, as explained in this book. But whether you are starting afresh or pivoting, one thing is for sure:

– *Nothing changes if nothing changes (Donna Barnes).*

You must be willing to take that next step into your future, whether this means spending an hour every day mastering a new skill, going back to school, or sharing your talent with the world. What's that first step for you?

I know that the thought of starting a new journey can be scary. My friend was scared for a long time. I was scared to the point that I almost went back to investment consulting just to play it safe. Most people feel the same way – letting go of familiarity is tough.

> *But is that fear worth getting to the end of your life, having lived a life that did not fulfill you?*
>
> *Is it worth waking up every day feeling like you are betraying yourself?*
>
> *Is it worth seeing other people living your dreams and wishing you had the courage to do the same?*

Knowing how it feels to lead an unfulfilling life, do not let that fear be the reason you keep holding back. Instead, act in the face of fear, in spite of it, because that fear won't just dissipate magically. It only goes away once you have put in the work, seen that you are capable of more than you could ever have imagined, and worked on your subconscious beliefs. And that's the beauty of pursuing ikigai with kaizen – it eats at that fear one bit at a time. You don't have to turn your life around in one go. You just start small by doing simple yet practical things. And as they add up and you start seeing their results, you get the courage and motivation to challenge yourself to try something just a little more daring. Then, some more, and before you know it, you're actually living the dream that you always wanted.

CHAPTER 8: THE 21-DAY PLAN TO MASTER YOUR IKIGAI WITH KAIZEN

This book gives you the tools you need to work through the challenges you may face along the way. Use these resources to map the rest of your life, creating the kind of life you want so that your vision board can become a reality. I'm not saying that it will be easy – however, it will be worth it. Once again, I will quote Henry Ford –

"Whether you think you can or you can't, you are right."

No matter how scared you may be of the future, start believing in yourself now by committing to the 21-day plan and taking that small first step. Don't worry about tomorrow or next week, or even a year from now. Just do what you need to do today, and that's enough.

Over time, you will see the benefits that small changes can have on your life. And then you can be a living testament to the fact that everyone can change their life by adjusting their approaches and their perspectives. Share your experiences with those around you so you can inspire them to be better. I think we can all agree that the world would be a happier place if people followed their passions and inspired others through their actions. Be that shining light for your loved ones as you work your way to embracing the "moai" concept for a better and thriving community.

Are you ready for your purposeful future? As you start this amazing journey, I leave you with this quote by James Clear:

"Every action you take is a vote for the type of person you wish to become."

YOUR JOURNEY DOESN'T END HERE!

Ikigai is not just a concept—it's a lifelong practice. Now that you've explored its foundations, it's time to bring these insights into your **everyday life**.

To help you stay on track, I've prepared an **exclusive workbook** packed with tools to refine your goals, track progress, and create a **clear roadmap for your future.**

Scan the QR code now or follow the link and take the next step toward a **life of clarity, purpose, and continuous growth!**

https://personalgrowthpages.com/winston-ikigai-workbook

THANK YOU!

I want to express my deepest gratitude to you for choosing to read my book. It brings me immense joy and satisfaction to know that my work has reached your hands. I hope it has provided you with valuable insights and knowledge.

As a small independent author, knowing that my words inspire and resonate with readers like you is always gratifying. Your support and enthusiasm for my book mean a lot to me.

I have a small favor to ask you: Would you be willing to help me if it only took less than 1 minute of your time?

If so, fantastic! All I need is for you to leave an honest review on Amazon for this book. Even though it takes less than a minute, your review can make a huge difference.

Your feedback could help someone discover their true purpose, build meaningful habits, and create a life of balance and fulfillment. By sharing your thoughts, you might inspire another person to embrace Ikigai, apply Kaizen, and take small steps toward lasting happiness. To keep it quick and easy, follow the link below or scan a QR code with your phone's camera and follow the link that pops up to go directly to your Amazon review page:

https://www.amazon.com/review/
create-review?&asin=B0DW9J9L5Q

If you prefer not to use the links, you can go to your Amazon orders page, find this book, scroll down to the reviews section, and click the "Write a review" option.

Thank you from the bottom of my heart for your time. Your support means the world to me.

REFERENCES

1. Apollo Technical LLC. (2024, September 17). *17 Remarkable Career Change Statistics To Know.* https://www.apollotechnical.com/career-change-statistics/
2. Benavidez, G. A., Zahnd, W. E., Hung, P., & Eberth, J. M. (2024). Chronic Disease Prevalence in the US: Sociodemographic and Geographic Variations by Zip Code Tabulation Area. *Preventing Chronic Disease, 21.* https://doi.org/10.5888/pcd21.230267
3. Bilodeau, K. (2019, November 28). *Will a purpose-driven life help you live longer?* Harvard Health. https://www.health.harvard.edu/blog/will-a-purpose-driven-life-help-you-live-longer-2019112818378
4. CDC. (2024, May 15). *About Emotional Well-Being.* Emotional Well-Being. https://www.cdc.gov/emotional-well-being/about/index.html
5. Earls, A. (2024, January 12). *Americans' Views of Life's Meaning and Purpose Are Changing.* Lifeway Research. https://research.lifeway.com/2021/04/06/americans-views-of-lifes-meaning-and-purpose-are-changing/
6. Johnson, S. (2023, November 17). WHO declares loneliness a 'global public health concern.' *The Guardian.* https://www.theguardian.com/global-development/2023/nov/16/who-declares-loneliness-a-global-public-health-concern

7. Lally, P., Van Jaarsveld, C. H., Potts, H. W., & Wardle, J. (2010). **How are habits formed: Modelling habit formation in the real world**. *European Journal of Social Psychology, 40*(6), 998-1009. DOI:10.1002/ejsp.674

8. Li, C., MD. (2019, June 27). *3 Charts | A Sense of Purpose Helps You Live Longer | Visualized Science.* https://www.clearvuehealth.com/b/purpose-longevity-health/

9. Mejia, Z. (2017, November 21). *Harvard researchers say this mental shift will help you live a longer, healthier life.* CNBC. https://www.cnbc.com/2017/11/21/harvard-researchers-say-a-purpose-leads-to-longer-healthier-life.html

10. Ortiz-Ospina, E., & Roser, M. (2024, March 20). *Happiness and Life Satisfaction.* Our World in Data. https://ourworldindata.org/happiness-and-life-satisfaction

11. Ryall, J. (2022, June 12). Japan: What's behind Okinawans' falling life expectancy? *dw.com.* https://www.dw.com/en/japan-whats-behind-okinawans-falling-life-expectancy/a-62088176

12. Spinoza, J. (2024, March 19). *42 Time Management Statistics to Inspire Efficiency in 2024 - Zoomshift.* Zoomshift. https://www.zoomshift.com/blog/time-management-statistics/

13. World Economic Forum. (2024, September 10). *A sense of purpose could prolong your life.* https://www.weforum.org/stories/2019/05/a-sense-of-purpose-could-prolong-your-life/

Made in the USA
Middletown, DE
21 August 2025

12721698R00118